STECK-VAUGHN

American Government

Freedom, Rights, Responsibilities

Vivian Bernstein

STECK-VAUGHN
ELEMENTARY · SECONDARY · ADULT · LIBRARY
A Harcourt Company

www.steck-vaughn.com

About the Author

Vivian Bernstein has been a teacher in the New York City Public School System for a number of years. She received her Master of Arts degree from New York University. Bernstein is active with professional organizations in social studies, education, and reading. She is the author of *America's Story*, *World History and You*, *World Geography and You*, and *Decisions for Health*.

Acknowledgments

Pages 50–51 reprinted by permission of Joan Daves Agency. Copyright © 1963 by Martin Luther King, Jr.
Cover: © Owen Franken/Stock, Boston, (Capitol); © Comstock, (Liberty Bell); The Library of Congress, (Independence Hall); National Archives, (Declaration of Independence).
pp.6–7 The Library of Congress (Constitutional Convention)
p.6 National Archives (Constitution)
p.6 The Bettmann Archive (Jefferson)
p.6 © Owen Franken/Stock Boston (U.S. Capitol)
p.8 National Archives
p.9 © SCALA/Art Resource
p.11 North Wind Picture Archive (seal)
p.11 The Bettmann Archive
p.12 © Cary Wolinsky/Stock Boston
p.15 The Library of Congress
p.16 The Library of Congress
p.17 North Wind Picture Archives
p.18 The Library of Congress
p.19 The Bettmann Archive
p.22 The Library of Congress
p.23 Historical Pictures Service, Chicago (Morris)
p.23 Library of Congress (Franklin)
p.24 Independence National Historical Park Collection
p.25 Independence National Historical Park Collection
p.26 North Wind Picture Archives
p.27 The Library of Congress
p.28 North Wind Picture Archives
p.31 North Wind Picture Archives (Madison)
p.31 Virginia Historical Society
p.33 © Owen Franken/Stock Boston
p.34 National Archives
p.35 The Bettmann Archive
p.36 UPI/Bettmann Newsphotos
p.37 The Bettmann Archive
p.38 © Keith Jewell
p.42 National Archives
p.43 AP/Wide World
p.45 UPI/Bettmannn Newsphotos
p.46 The Library of Congress
p.47 The Bettmann Archive
p.50 UPI/Bettmann Newsphotos
p.51 UPI/Bettmann Newsphotos
pp.52–53 Reuters/Bettmann
p.52 White House Photos (Presidential Seal)
p.52 AP/Wide World (Capitol)
p.54 The Bettmann Archive
p.56 AP/Wide World
p.57 U.S. Senate Photo
p.58 UPI/Bettmann Newsphotos
p.59 Office of the Speaker, US Capitol
p.62 AP/Wide World
p.63 © Cynthia Johnson/Gamma-Liaison

p.64 LBJ Library
p.65 Reuters/Bettmann
p.66 © Robert Ward/Department of Defense
p.67 UPI/Bettmann Newsphotos
p.68 National Portrait Gallery
p.71 © Rob Lawlor/Philadelphia Daily News
p.72 AP/Wide World (portrait)
p.72 UPI/Bettmann Newsphotos (speech)
p.73 © Gale Zucker/Stock Boston
p.74 © Susan Biddle/White House Photos
p.75 © Diana Walker/Gamma-Liaison
p.80 NASA
p.81 © Terry Ashe/Gamma-Liaison
p.84 UPI/Bettmann Newsphotos
p.85 The Supreme Court Historical Society
p.86 © Trippett/Sipa Press
p.87 © Jim Pickerell/Stock Boston
p.88 The Bettmann Archive
p.89 UPI/Bettmann Newsphotos
p.92 © Trippett/Sipa Press
p.93 © Terry Ashe/Gamma-Liaison
p.95 AP/Wide World
p.96 © Terry Ashe/Gamma-Liaison
p.97 Reuters/Bettmann
p.102 © Carl Iwasaki/Life Magazine
p.103 © Jeffry Myers/Stock Boston
pp.104–105 © A.J. Hartman/Comstock
p.104 Virginia State Library (VA State Constitution)
p.104 © Rhoda Sidney/PhotoEdit (police officer)
p.104 © Charles Kennard/Stock Boston (CA Capitol)
p.106 © Kenneth Garrett/Woodfin Camp & Associates
p.107 © Paul Conklin/PhotoEdit
p.109 © Jim Pickerell/Stock Boston
p.110 © Barbara Rios/Photo Researchers
p.114 © Bob Daemmerich
p.115 © Van Bucher/Photo Researchers
p.116 © Leif Skoogfors/Woodfin Camp & Associates
p.117 UPI/Bettmann Newsphotos
p.118 © Bob Daemmerich
p.121 Reuters/Bettmann Newsphotos
p.122 © Jeffrey D. Smith/Woodfin Camp & Associates
p.123 © Tony Freeman/PhotoEdit
p.124 © Paul Sequeira/Photo Researchers
p.125 UPI/Bettmann Newsphotos
p.129 UPI/Bettmann Newsphotos (Harold Washington)
p.129 © Mark Segal/TSW-Click/Chicago (Chicago)
p.130 © David Young-Wolff/PhotoEdit
p.131 © Craig Aurness/Westlight
pp.132–133 UPI/Bettmann Newsphotos
p.132 © Michael Hayman/Stock Boston (voters)
p.132 The Bettmann Archive (JFK button)
p.132 UPI/Bettmann Newsphotos (buttons)

p.134 © Owen Franken/Stock Boston
p.135 © Ellis Herwig/Stock Boston
p.136 The Bettmann Archive
p.137 © Kenneth Jarecke/Woodfin Camp & Associates
p.138 © Phyllis Graber Jensen/Stock Boston
p.139 © Michael Hayman/Stock Boston
p.143 AP/Wide World
p.144 © Jacques Chenet/Woodfin Camp & Associates
p.145 © Bob McNeeley/The Democratic National Party
p.146 © John Chiason/Gamma-Liaison
p.147 UPI/Bettmann Newsphotos
p.148 UPI/Bettmann Newsphotos
p.149 © Tony Freeman/PhotoEdit
p.152 © Trippett, Witt/Sipa Press (speech)
p.152 © Diana Walker/Gamma-Liaison (Noonan)
p.153 AP/Wide World
p.154 © Terry Ashe/Gamma-Liaison
p.155 © Dirck Halstead/Gamma-Liaison
p.156 AP/Wide World
p.158 © John Troha/Black Star
p.162 Courtesy Senator Nancy Kassebaum
p.163 Kansans for Kassebaum
pp.164–165 Reuters/Bettmann
p.164 Texas Highway Department (flag)
p.164 © Isabel Cutler/Gamma-Liaison (U.S. Embassy)
p.166 © David Young-Wolff/PhotoEdit
p.167 © J. Myers/H. Armstrong Roberts
p.168 AP/Wide World
p.172 NASA
p.175 © Laimute Druskis/Stock Boston
p.176 © Paul Conklin/PhotoEdit
p.177 UPI/Bettmann Newsphotos
p.178 Reuters/Bettmann Newsphotos
p.179 AP/Wide World
p.182 Reuters/Bettmann Newsphotos
p.183 © Ron Sanford/Black Star
p.184 © P.O., T.F./PhotoEdit
p.185 © T. Graham/Sygma
p.186 AP/Wide World
p.187 AP/Wide World
p.191 AP/Wide World
p.192 © Allen Green/Photo Researchers
p.193 UPI/Bettmann Newsphotos
p.194 AP/Wide World
p.195 © James Foote/Photo Researchers
p.196 AP/Wide World
p.197 © Clifford/Gamma-Liaison
p.200 © Ed Gamble/Florida Times Union
p.201 National Portrait Gallery (portrait)
p.201 AP/Wide World (Habitat for Humanity)
p.202 National Portrait Gallery
p.203 UPI/Bettmann Newsphotos

Consultant:

Alexandra M. Dailey teaches government and American history in Austin, TX.

Staff Credits:

Executive Editor: Diane Sharpe
Design Manager: Cynthia Ellis
Photo Editor: Margie Foster
Production: Go Media, Inc.

ISBN 0-8172-6343-8

14 15 16 17 18 19 20 21 073 11 10 09 08 07 06 05 04

Table of Contents

To the Reader

President Abraham Lincoln once said that we have a government "of the people, by the people, for the people." What did he mean by that?

Our government was formed by a group of men who were chosen by the people of the new United States. They worked together for many long days to design a government for their new nation. They wanted the new government to meet the needs of all the people. They also wanted the government to be run by the people.

The government touches your life in many ways. On the day you were born your parents filled out forms to let the government know that you had arrived. When you entered school you were taking advantage of a government service. Taxes that are taken out of your paycheck go to pay for government services.

You touch the government's life every time you vote. When you write to your leaders, you are taking part in government.

American Government tells the story of how our government came to be. You will learn about all the branches of the government and their many jobs. You will see how leaders are elected, and how people like you can make a difference. You will learn about the role our government plays as one nation among many. You will see that your government is "of the people, by the people, for the people."

At the end of the book you will find two important pieces of writing. The first, the Declaration of Independence, is the letter written to the King of England. It tells him that the people of the United States wanted to be free. The second, the Constitution of the United States, is the group of laws that tell how our government is put together and run. Along with these great pieces of writing is an explanation that will help you to understand what those papers mean.

As you read this book and those two papers, think about how the government is important to you. Think also about how important you are to the government.

UNIT 1
Government for a New Nation

In 1776, Americans told the world they wanted to be free from rule by Great Britain. But Great Britain was not eager to let its colonies go. So Americans and British fought in the American Revolution. When this fight for freedom ended, the new nation of the United States needed a government of its own. American leaders met and wrote a plan of government. That plan is explained in the Constitution of the United States.

The Preamble, or beginning, of the Constitution sets the goals for the government of the United States. It tells us that the government will protect and defend the people of the United States. It says that the government will work for peace and for the good of the people.

The Constitution was signed in 1787. It has served as a guide for our government for over two hundred years.

Have You Ever Wondered . . .

- Great Britain had a king. Why doesn't the United States have one?

- At one time, every state made its own money. States don't anymore. Why not?

- The men who wrote the Constitution used ideas from the Greeks, the Romans, and the British. Why?

- Unfair taxes were one reason Americans fought for freedom from Great Britain. How could taxes cause a war?

- Some men who wrote the Constitution had slaves. Others did not. How did slavery affect the way our government was created?

All of those questions will be answered in this unit. You will read about how the Constitution came to be written, who helped write it, and what ideas the writers had about how their government should be formed. You will learn why Americans wanted their own form of government and how they made their government different from that of Great Britain. You will read about the government these leaders created, how it is run, and by whom. As you read this unit, think about why the Constitution has worked so well for more than two hundred years.

Chapter 1

Building a New Nation

Consider As You Read

• Why is a government important for a new nation?
• Which ideas from other nations were used to plan our government?

government
system of rule

In 1776, a new nation was born. But that nation had no **government.** Eleven years passed before leaders created a government they felt would work. In 1787, forty men signed the Constitution of the United States of America. The Constitution describes the government those leaders created. For over two hundred years that government has been at work.

Why do we need government? Imagine living in a city that did not have a government. Living in a city without a government might sound like fun, but life would be filled with problems. There would be no laws against stealing, so many robberies would take place each day. There would be no rules for driving cars. Even young children might drive! Who would protect people from robbers and unsafe drivers? Who would decide if the city needed fire fighters, garbage collectors, police, and teachers? To help people live together peacefully and safely, governments are needed.

Today people can see the Constitution in Washington, D.C.

In Rome, representatives for the people worked in the government.

Every nation, and every state, city, and town within a nation, needs a government. All the people who make laws and carry out the laws for an area are part of the government. In the United States, the President, lawmakers, and judges are part of the government.

Early Ideas About Democracy

In 1776, the leaders of the United States wanted their government to be a democracy. The word **democracy** comes from Greek. It means "rule by the people." In a democracy, people vote for their leaders and lawmakers. People in our democracy have the right to speak, vote, write, and pray as they wish.

Democracy was not a new idea in 1776. The world's first democracy started more than two thousand years ago in Greece. In Athens, Greece, all citizens were allowed to vote. The citizens of Athens worked together at large meetings to make the city's laws. All citizens of Athens had the same rights. But fewer than half of the people of Athens were allowed to be citizens. Women, slaves, and people who were not born in Athens could not be citizens.

democracy
government in which the people rule

The democracy of Athens was a direct democracy. In a direct democracy, all citizens work and vote together at city meetings. All citizens help write new laws together. Direct democracy works best in a city with a small population. Direct democracy worked in Athens because the city did not have a large population.

In 1787, American leaders knew that their nation was too large for direct democracy. They also knew they did not want a king. Instead, the United States would need a representative government. In a representative government, people vote for leaders to **represent** them. These elected leaders work together to make laws for the nation. The world's first representative government began 2,500 years ago in the city of Rome. Romans voted for **representatives** to make laws for them. Hundreds of years later, Great Britain began to use the Roman ideas about representative government.

represent
speak or act for

representatives
people chosen to speak or act for others

Representative Government Grows in Great Britain

Americans learned from Great Britain how representative democracy could work. The Magna Carta was Great Britain's first step toward representative government. The Magna Carta was an important paper that the nation's king, King John, was forced to sign in the year 1215. For many years, King John

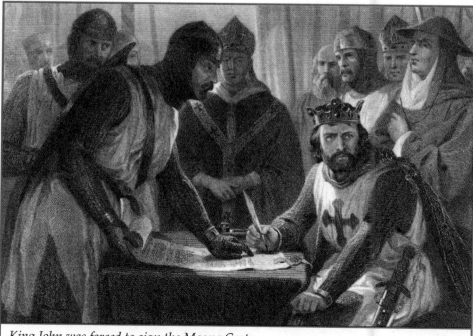

King John was forced to sign the Magna Carta.

10

The Magna Carta changed government in Great Britain.

King John's seal

forced the nobles, who were leaders under King John, to pay many taxes. In 1215, a group of angry nobles wrote the Magna Carta because they wanted the king to obey the laws of the land. The Magna Carta said that the king, like everyone else in Great Britain, now had to obey the nation's laws. The Magna Carta was important because it limited the king's power. A nation could have a representative government only if the king shared his power with the lawmakers.

The Magna Carta was also important because it gave accused people the right to a **trial** by a **jury** of **peers.** For hundreds of years, kings had sent people who disagreed with them to prison. If people did have a trial, the jury was made up only of nobles. The Magna Carta said that every accused person must be tried by a jury of peers. For example, at the trial of an accused working person, the people of the jury must be other working people.

After the Magna Carta, representative government slowly grew stronger in Great Britain. A group of lawmakers called **Parliament** began to help the king write laws. These lawmakers represented the nobles. At first, only rich nobles were allowed to vote for representatives in Parliament. Only rich nobles were allowed to work in Parliament. As the years

trial
event where a person accused of a crime is judged

jury
group of people who decide whether or not an accused person has committed a crime

peers
equals

Parliament
group of lawmakers in Great Britain

passed, more and more men were allowed to vote and become lawmakers in Parliament. Everyone, including the king, had to obey the laws made by Parliament.

The English Bill of Rights of 1689 strengthened representative government and democracy in Great Britain. The Bill of Rights gave Parliament the power to make most of Great Britain's laws. Only Parliament could write tax laws. Parliament had much more power than the king. The Bill of Rights also protected the rights of the people. It allowed people to speak and write against the government. There was more freedom in Great Britain than in most European nations.

The Magna Carta and the Bill of Rights helped Great Britain become a parliamentary government. In Britain today, a parliamentary government still rules. In this type of government, Parliament, not the king or queen, makes the nation's laws. Parliament has two houses. Nobles work in Parliament's House of Lords. Representatives are elected to the House of Commons. The leader of Parliament is the nation's **prime minister.** The prime minister is Britain's leader and must carry out the laws that Parliament passes.

When American leaders met to write the Constitution, they thought about what they had learned about democracy and representative government from the Greeks, Romans, and British. They would use this knowledge to plan a new kind of government for the American nation.

prime minister
leader of a parliamentary government

Parliament meets in this building in London, England.

12

Using What You Learned

Comprehension — *Who Said It?*

Read each statement. Then look in the box for the person who might have said it. Write the name of the person you choose on the blank after each sentence.

British Prime Minister	**Citizen of Athens**
Citizen of Rome	**King John**

1. "The best government is a direct democracy where all citizens make the laws."

   _____

2. "I will vote for lawmakers to represent me in the government."

   _____

3. "As the leader of Parliament, I must carry out its laws."

   _____

4. "Since the nobles want me to obey the law, they are forcing me to sign the Magna Carta."

   _____

Vocabulary — *Match Up*

Choose a word or phrase in the box to complete each sentence. Write that word or phrase on the blank.

parliamentary government	representatives	jury
democracy	population	citizen
Parliament	prime minister	

1. In a _____ the people rule.

2. _____ is the number of people who live in an area.

3. A _____ enjoys all the rights of a nation.

4. In a trial the _____ decides whether the accused person is innocent or guilty.

5. In a _____ laws are made by representatives of Parliament.

6. _____ are elected to represent the people.

7. In Great Britain, lawmakers belong to _____ .

8. The _____ is the leader of a parliamentary government.

Critical Thinking — *Categories*

Read the words in each group. Decide how they are alike. Write a title for each group on the blank beside each group. You may use the words in the box as part or all of each title.

representative Magna Carta	Bill of Rights government	democracy Parliament

1. King John
   1215
   limited power

   _____

2. Athens
   vote
   citizens

   _____

3. tax laws by Parliament
   free speech
   protected rights

   _____

4. House of Lords
   House of Commons
   prime minister

   _____

5. Romans
   elect
   representatives

   _____

Chapter 2

Early Governments in the United States

Consider As You Read
- How did experiences with colonial governments help Americans plan a new government for the nation?
- Why did Americans want their independence?

American leaders wanted to plan a representative government for their young nation. The government would be a democracy in which people would make laws to protect the rights and freedom of the people. These leaders had many ideas about government from their work in the governments of the thirteen colonies. They used what they learned from the colonial governments to plan a new and different kind of government for the United States.

Colonial Governments

By the year 1753, Great Britain ruled thirteen colonies in America. Because the colonies were ruled by Great Britain, all colonists, including the colonial governors and lawmakers, had to obey the laws of Parliament. But all of the thirteen colonial governments were representative governments.

Representatives for the colonists worked in their government.

colonists
people living in colonies

legislature
lawmaking body

executive
leader

governor
leader of a colony or state

natural rights
rights belonging to every person

liberty
freedom

Colonists voted for representatives to write their laws in the **legislature.** An **executive,** called the **governor,** was the leader of each colony. Most of the time, the governor was chosen by the British king. But in two colonies, colonists voted for their own governors.

Democracy in the thirteen colonial governments was similar in some ways to democracy in Great Britain. Accused people were given jury trials to decide if they should be punished and sent to jail. Every colony had a limited government, a government where the leaders did not have full power and had to obey the laws.

Many colonists believed in the idea of **natural rights.** These include the right to life, **liberty,** and property. Leaders in the colonies wanted the government to protect the natural rights of all people. They felt that a democracy would help to protect these rights.

Free elections helped the growth of democracy in the colonies. In every colony men who owned land could vote. It was much easier to buy and own land in the colonies than in Great Britain, so far more people were allowed to vote in the colonies than in Great Britain.

Revolution and Independence

In 1760, King George became Britain's new king. George was only 22 years old when he became king, and he knew little about life in the American colonies. King George soon realized that Great Britain needed more money. Britain had spent large amounts of money fighting a long war in North America against France. After Britain won that war in 1763, King George decided that the colonies should give Britain some of the money Britain needed. So Parliament wrote tax laws for the colonies. The Stamp Act was one of those laws. This law forced colonists to pay new taxes on all newspapers, books, and even playing cards.

Colonists were angry about the Stamp Act and other British tax laws. They felt these laws were unfair because the colonies were not allowed to send representatives to Parliament to help write the laws. The colonists did not want to obey laws that they were not allowed to help write. But the British refused to allow colonial representatives in Parliament. They

King George

16

After winning the war, George Washington led his army into New York City.

also continued to write laws that angered the colonists. One of these laws forced Americans to allow British soldiers to sleep in their homes. After angry colonists threw tea into Boston Harbor, another law closed the harbor so the colonists could not use it for trade. Colonists complained that they did not have the right to decide their own laws.

In 1774, representatives from twelve colonies formed the First Continental Congress in Philadelphia. This was very bold, since they were making decisions without help from Great Britain. Because the colonists were angry about the unfair tax laws, they decided to stop all trade with Great Britain. If their problems with King George continued, they would meet again in one year.

The problems with Great Britain grew worse because Parliament continued to write laws that angered the colonists. In 1775, colonists were so unhappy with King George and the British Parliament that they formed their own army. In that year, American soldiers began to fight the British for the rights they thought the British were taking away. The American Revolution had begun!

In 1775, **delegates** from all thirteen colonies met again at the Second Continental Congress in Philadelphia. The delegates decided they did not want the colonies to be ruled by Great Britain. They wanted the colonies to be an **independent** nation. The men at the Congress asked one of the delegates, Thomas Jefferson, to write a paper that explained why the colonies needed their freedom.

With help from others, Thomas Jefferson wrote the Declaration of Independence. He told the world why the

delegates
people who are chosen to represent others

independent
free and not relying on another

17

colonies wanted to be a free and independent nation. This important paper said that all people have the natural rights to live, be free, and make a living. Since King George had tried to take away these rights, the colonies would no longer be ruled by Great Britain. The Declaration also said that a government gets its power from the people and must work for the people. These ideas would later be used to plan the new government for the United States.

However, Great Britain did not want its American colonies to become a free nation. Britain needed the colonies for trade. The British earned money by selling many kinds of products to the colonies. So Britain sent soldiers to fight against the Americans. At last in 1781, Americans won their war for freedom. The thirteen colonies became an independent nation, the United States of America.

The Articles of Confederation

During the American Revolution, men at the Second Continental Congress wrote the nation's first plan of government. They called this plan the Articles of Confederation. Finally, after four years, all thirteen states had **ratified** the Articles of Confederation. In 1781, the Articles of Confederation became the nation's first plan of government.

The Articles of Confederation gave most of the power to make laws to the states. So the central government had very little power. A central government is a government that controls all the state governments. Most Americans wanted the central government to have little power. They remembered how the British government used its power to take away the

ratified
approved

Thomas Jefferson (seated, left) and Benjamin Franklin (standing, left) were two signers of the Declaration of Independence.

The Articles of Confederation were written at the Second Continental Congress.

colonies' rights and freedom. To be sure the new government could not do the same thing, they planned a central government with very few powers.

The new central government had a legislature called Congress. Every state, large or small, had just one vote in Congress. Congress had no power over the thirteen states, and it could not collect taxes from the states. The Articles of Confederation did not give the central government an executive, so there was no leader to carry out the laws.

Soon people realized that the new government had many weaknesses. Congress did not have the power to force the states to obey its laws. Each state printed its own money. This was confusing because the money of one state could not be used in another state. Since Congress could not collect taxes, the central government had very little money. It did not even have enough money to pay for an army to protect the nation. While most people felt that they were citizens of the states, they did not feel like citizens of one large nation.

By 1787, many Americans wanted changes in their government. They thought the United States would not remain an independent nation unless it had a different kind of government. Many people feared that other nations would try to take control of the United States. In 1787, delegates from twelve states met again in Philadelphia to improve the Articles of Confederation. The thirteenth state, Rhode Island, did not want a stronger central government, and it refused to send delegates to Philadelphia. Delegates from the other states soon decided to plan a new and different kind of government. In the next chapter, you will learn how these delegates planned a government that has lasted more than two hundred years.

Comprehension — *Write a Paragraph*

Use six or more words or phrases in the box to write a paragraph that tells how and why the American colonies became an independent nation.

Declaration of Independence	**Parliament**	**taxes**
American Revolution	**King George**	**representatives**
natural rights	**freedom**	

_____

_____

_____

_____

_____

_____

Vocabulary — *Find the Meaning*

Write the word or phrase that best completes each sentence on the blank.

1. A member of a **legislature** helps make _____ .

    laws   jobs   freedom

2. When a government protects the **natural rights** of the people, the people enjoy

    _____ .

    taxes   jobs   freedom

3. An **executive** might be a _____ .

    judge   congress   governor

4. The **delegates** at the Continental Congress_____ their states.

    represented   elected   ratified

5. An **independent** nation _____ .

      rules itself   has no government   is ruled by another nation

6. When states **ratify** laws, they _____ them.

      disapprove   approve   obey

Critical Thinking — *Cause and Effect*

A **cause** is something that makes something else happen. What happens is called the **effect.**

    Cause: King George made unfair laws.
    Effect: Americans were angry with Britain.

Choose a cause or an effect from **Group B** to complete each sentence in **Group A**. Write the letter of the correct answer on the blank. The first one is done for you.

Group A

1. ___**b**___, so more men could vote in the colonies.

2. In 1774, Americans were unhappy with British laws, so _____ .

3. Americans wanted Britain to know they no longer wanted to be ruled by Britain, so _____ .

4. Americans didn't want the new government to take away their rights, so _____ .

5. _____, so there was not enough money to pay for an army.

6. _____, so they fought to keep their colonies.

Group B

a. The Articles of Confederation gave few powers to the central government.

b. It was easier to own land in America than in Britain.

c. They stopped all trade with Britain.

d. The British wanted trade in America.

e. Thomas Jefferson wrote the Declaration of Independence.

f. Congress could not collect taxes.

Chapter 3

Writing the Constitution

Consider As You Read
- Who wrote the Constitution?
- What important ideas did the Framers share?
- How did the Framers work together to write the Constitution?

To improve the Articles of Confederation, 55 men came to Philadelphia in May of 1787. They came from twelve of the thirteen states, and they met to correct the problems in their government. Before long, the delegates realized that there were too many problems with the Articles of Confederation. The nation needed a better plan of government. During the next four months, the delegates wrote a new constitution for the nation. Those laws, the United States Constitution, are the highest laws of the land. They have guided our nation for more than two hundred years.

The Constitution of the United States was signed in 1787.

Planning a New Constitution

The 55 men who wrote the Constitution in 1787 were called the Framers of the Constitution. They were chosen by their states to be representatives to the meeting in Philadelphia. This meeting is now called the Constitutional Convention.

The men at the convention were farmers, lawyers, and merchants. Many had fought in the American Revolution. Who were some of the most important Framers? George Washington had been commander in chief of the colonial army during the American Revolution, and Americans everywhere loved and respected him. All of the delegates voted for Washington to be president of the convention. Benjamin Franklin, at 81, was the oldest delegate. Franklin helped write the Declaration of Independence and had convinced the French to help the colonies during the American Revolution. James Madison was the first person to arrive at the convention. He brought more useful ideas to the convention than any other delegate. Gouverneur Morris was known for being a good writer. At the end of the convention, Morris rewrote all the ideas into the beautiful language of the Constitution.

Gouverneur Morris

The Framers decided that everything said at the convention would be kept secret. Although the convention was held during the hot summer months, all windows and doors were kept tightly shut during the meetings. The convention lasted almost four months, and during that time, newspapers could not write reports about the convention. No one was allowed to discuss the problems and decisions of the daily meetings with people who were not at the convention. Why were the meetings kept a secret? The Framers wanted to speak freely. In secrecy, they could argue with each other and speak about their ideas because no one outside the convention would know what was said.

Benjamin Franklin

Agreements and Arguments

All of the Framers agreed on six important ideas for the new Constitution. These ideas were used to plan a representative democracy where the people would rule and make fair laws for the nation. The Framers believed that a government based on these six ideas would not be able to take away freedom and liberty from the people Instead, the government would protect the rights of the people, and still have enough power to control the states.

What were the six ideas that the Framers used to write the Constitution? First, they all believed that the Constitution had to protect the natural rights of the people to life, liberty, and property. Second, they believed in limited government. The powers of government would be controlled by law, and everyone would have to obey the law. Third, they believed in **popular sovereignty.** This means government gets its power from the people. People would vote for leaders and lawmakers.

The fourth idea was called the **separation of powers.** This means that the powers of government are divided among three branches. These branches are the executive, the **legislative,** and the **judicial.** Separation of powers prevents one part of the government from becoming so powerful it can take away the freedom of the people. For example, the separation of powers limits the power of a President by not

popular sovereignty
rule by the people

separation of powers
the power is split among different branches of government

legislative
lawmaking

judicial
made up of judges

The Constitutional Convention met in Independence Hall, Philadelphia.

Today many people visit Independence Hall, where the Constitution was signed.

allowing the President to write laws. Each of the three branches has its own powers, and the branches must work together to govern the nation.

Checks and balances was the fifth idea the Framers agreed on. This means each branch of government checks on, or limits, the power of the other branches. The power of each branch balances the power of the others. For example, the judges decide if the laws that Congress writes follow the ideas in the Constitution. Checks and balances limit the power of each branch of government.

Sixth, the Framers believed in **federalism.** This means they wanted a central, or federal, government that would share power with the states. The federal and state governments would have different powers. For example, only the federal government can print money, and only state governments can make marriage laws. Other powers, such as making taxes, are shared by the federal and state governments.

Compromises

The delegates often disagreed about how these ideas should be carried out in the Constitution. They disagreed about how Congress should be organized. They disagreed about the number of representatives each state should send to Congress. The Framers solved many problems through **compromise.** Even today democracy only works because people in the

checks and balances
each branch of government keeps the others from gaining too much power

federalism
government in which power is divided between a central government and state governments

compromise
giving in on each side in order to reach agreement

branches of government compromise with each other. A strong, powerful leader cannot make all decisions and laws in a democracy. Instead, government leaders and lawmakers compromise in order to reach agreements about the best laws and programs for the nation. What were some of the compromises at the Constitutional Convention?

The first compromise was about representation in Congress. All of the Framers wanted the United States to have a representative government. Representatives from every state would make laws in Congress. The states with large populations wanted more representatives in Congress than the states with smaller populations wanted. Because the larger states had more people, they thought they should have more power in Congress. The smaller states wanted every state to send the same number of representatives to Congress. These states wanted to be sure that they would have enough representation in Congress to protect their own interests. The delegates reached a compromise. There would be two houses, or parts, in Congress. One house, the Senate, would have two **senators** from every state. In this house, large and small states would have equal representation and equal power. The other

senators
representatives in the Senate

For almost four months, leaders discussed how to create a new government.

George Washington was our first President.

house, the House of Representatives, would have more representatives from states with large populations. Smaller states would have fewer representatives. Because this was the most important compromise made during the Convention, it was called the Great Compromise.

The delegates also compromised about the question of slavery. There were many slaves in the southern states. The southern states wanted slaves to be counted as part of their population for representation in Congress. The northern states disagreed because counting slaves for representation would give the southern states more power in Congress. The delegates reached a compromise. Not all slaves, but three fifths of the slaves, would be counted as part of the population for representation in Congress. This compromise was called the Three-Fifths Compromise.

Still another compromise about slavery was needed. Many slaves were brought into the nation from Africa. Landowners in the southern states depended on these slaves to do plantation work, but slavery was not allowed in some northern states. Southerners were afraid the Congress would make laws to stop the slave trade. The Framers reached a compromise by deciding that no laws could be written to stop the slave trade for twenty years.

Signatures on the Constitution

amendments
laws added to the Constitution

ratification
approval

majority
at least more than half

Other Decisions for the Constitution

The Framers made many more decisions as they planned the Constitution. They decided that a president would lead the executive branch. They decided how long senators and representatives could serve in Congress. The Framers also wrote about federalism. They decided which powers would belong to the federal government and which to the state governments. Only the federal government could have an army and go to war against other nations. State governments could make laws about school. The Framers also knew that, as the nation grew and changed, more laws would be needed. So one part of the Constitution explains how new laws, called **amendments,** can be added.

Ratification

In September 1787, the Framers finished writing the Constitution. The Constitution had to be ratified by nine states before it could become the nation's law. Back in 1777, all thirteen states were needed to ratify the Articles of Confederation. The Framers remembered that it had taken four years before all thirteen states ratified the Articles of Confederation. They wanted the Constitution ratified quickly because the nation needed the new government. Because it would be difficult to get all thirteen states to ratify the Constitution quickly, they decided that nine states were enough for **ratification.** Nine states were a clear **majority.** In a democracy, decisions are usually made by the majority.

Each state held meetings to decide about ratification of the Constitution. Many people liked the strong federal government created in the Constitution. Others at these meetings were unhappy with the Constitution because they thought it gave too much power to the federal government. These people felt the Constitution needed a Bill of Rights to protect the rights of the people, so the Framers promised that a Bill of Rights would be added. At last, in 1788, the Constitution was ratified. People all over the nation celebrated its approval.

Comprehension — *Reviewing Important Facts*

Match the sentence in **Group A** with the word or phrase from **Group B** that the sentence explains. Write the letter of the correct answer on the blank.

Group A

_____ 1. These people wrote the Constitution.

_____ 2. Government should get its power from the people.

_____ 3. The federal and state governments share power.

_____ 4. The power of government is in three branches.

_____ 5. The branches of government limit each other's power.

Group B

a. popular sovereignty

b. separation of power

c. federalism

d. Framers

e. checks and balances

Vocabulary — *Writing With Vocabulary Words*

Use six or more words in the box to write a paragraph that tells about important ideas in the Constitution.

compromises	popular sovereignty	representation
separation of powers	amendments	checks and balances
judicial	executive	legislative

_____

_____

_____

_____

_____

Critical Thinking — *Analogies*

An **analogy** compares two pairs of words. The words in the first pair are alike in the same way as the words in the second pair. For example, Washington, D.C., is to the United States as Albany is to New York. Washington, D.C., is the capital of the United States just as Albany is the capital of New York. Use a word in the box to finish each sentence. You will not use all the words in the box.

Framers	federal	senators	Constitution
federalism	judges	states	Senate

1. Representatives are to the House of Representatives as senators are to the

   _____ .

2. The President is to the executive branch as _____ are to the judicial branch.

3. State governments are to the states as _____ government is to the nation.

4. 1776 is to the Declaration of Independence as 1787 is to the

   _____ .

5. Printing money is to the federal government as marriage laws are to the

   _____ .

Critical Thinking — *Fact or Opinion*

Read each sentence below. If the sentence is a fact, write **F** on the blank. If the sentence is an opinion, write **O** on the blank. If the sentence gives both a fact and an opinion, write **FO** on the blank and circle the part of the sentence that is an opinion.

_____ 1. George Washington was chosen to be the president of the Constitutional Convention.

_____ 2. There are three natural rights protected in the Constitution, and the most important one is the right to property.

_____ 3. It is better to have two senators from each state than to have three.

_____ 4. The Three-Fifths Compromise was made because states disagreed about counting slaves for representation.

_____ 5. The Constitution was ratified in 1788 by a clear majority of the states.

James Madison (1751–1836)

James Madison

James Madison was often called the great little Madison by his friends. This short, thin, quiet man did as much to shape the Constitution as any other representative at the Constitutional Convention.

James Madison was born in Virginia in 1751. He helped write a Constitution and a Bill of Rights for his state of Virginia. His work for Virginia prepared him for becoming one of the Framers of the Constitution.

The other Framers listened carefully to Madison's ideas as they argued about the shape of their new government. They respected Madison for his knowledge and good sense. Madison was able to lead the Framers to compromise on many ideas. When the Constitution was finished, Madison and 37 others signed it.

After signing the Constitution, Madison began to work for its ratification. He and two others wrote newspaper articles that explained why the Constitution would be good for the nation. They helped persuade people to ratify the new Constitution. These articles were put into a book called *The Federalist Papers.* This book is one of the most important books about government ever written.

No other American did as much as James Madison to plan and write the Constitution. He earned the title "Father of the Constitution."

James Madison built this house in Virginia.

Skill Builder

Reading a Line Graph

A **line graph** uses lines to show how something changes over time. A line graph also shows if there is a **trend** to the change. That is, does the line mostly go up over a certain time, or does it go down? The line graph below shows how the number of representatives from New York and California has changed over time. Look at the line graph. Then write the answer to each question.

The Number of Representatives from New York and California, 1940–1990

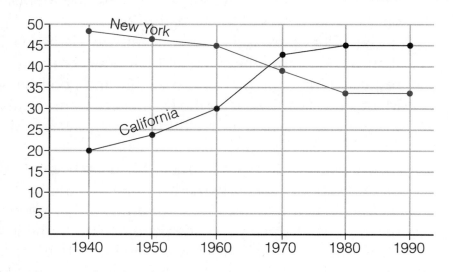

1. How many representatives did California have in 1940? _____

   In 1990? _____

2. Describe the trend in California from 1940 to 1980. _____

   _____

3. Describe what happened to the number of representatives from each state from 1960

   to 1970. _____

4. In what way is the trend from 1980 to 1990 in both states alike?

   _____

5. What can you say about the populations of New York and California from 1940

   to 1990 by looking at this graph? _____

   _____

Chapter 4

Understanding Our Constitution

Consider As You Read

- What powers does each branch of government have?
- Why are the powers of government separated among three branches?
- How does the Constitution protect the rights and freedom of the people?

The Framers of the Constitution had several goals as they planned the nation's government. They wanted the new government to be strong enough to rule the nation, but to get its power from the people. The powers of government had to be limited, and the natural rights of the people had to be protected. Another goal was to create a flexible constitution that could be used as the nation grew and changed. They did not want the United States ever to need another constitution. As you read this chapter, think about the ways the Constitution has met these important goals.

Representatives to the United States government work in the Capitol.

The Constitution Has Eight Parts

Preamble
introduction to the Constitution

document
piece of writing

justice
fairness; rightness

articles
sections

The Constitution starts with the **Preamble.** The Preamble states the goals of this important **document.** "We the people of the United States . . . " are the first words of the Preamble. From the start, the Framers wanted everyone to know that the people of the United States were planning a democratic nation. The Preamble tells us that **justice**, peace, safety, and liberty are the goals for American government.

The first seven **articles** of the Constitution follow the Preamble. Articles 1, 2, and 3 describe the way the government works. Articles 4 through 7 describe other important ideas.

Article 1 explains how the legislature, or Congress, should work. It limits the powers of Congress and the powers of state governments.

Article 2 describes the powers of the executive branch.

Article 3 explains the powers of the judicial branch.

Article 4 describes how states must cooperate with each other.

Article 5 explains how amendments can be added to the Constitution.

Article 6 is the Supremacy Law. This means every state must obey the Constitution. It is the highest law of the nation. Every President, judge, member of Congress, as well as other government **officials,** must swear to obey the Constitution.

officials
people holding offices

Article 7 explains how the Constitution must be ratified in order to become the law of the nation.

Separation of Powers

The Framers of the Constitution wanted to protect the rights and freedom of Americans. They remembered how King George and the British Parliament had taken away the rights and freedom of the colonists. To make sure the American government would never take away the rights of the people, the Framers divided power among three different branches of government. The Constitution gives separate powers to the legislative, the executive, and the judicial branches. Together, the three branches have enough power to govern the nation and also protect the rights of Americans. The chart on page 41 shows the powers that belong to each of the three branches.

The Preamble to the Constitution

34

Edmund Randolph (first from right), Thomas Jefferson, Alexander Hamilton, and Henry Knox were George Washington's Cabinet.

Article 1 of the Constitution explains the powers of Congress, the lawmaking branch. Congress is the voice of the people because all of its members are elected by the people. The people of each state elect senators and representatives who will make the nation's laws. The two houses of Congress must work together to pass laws.

The executive branch, led by the President of the United States, carries out the laws passed by Congress. In Article 2 of the Constitution, the powers of the President are explained. The President plans programs to enforce the laws. Many people help the President plan ways to carry out the laws of Congress. Article 2 also states that the President is **commander in chief** of the Army and Navy. This means that the President leads all branches of the military.

What are some ways the executive branch carries out the laws passed by the legislature? Congress can **declare war** against another nation, but the President, with his advisers, will decide how that war should be fought. During a war, the executive branch decides how many members of the armed forces must fight, when and where they should fight, and what kinds of weapons they should use. The collection of tax money is another example of the way the executive branch enforces the laws of Congress. Tax laws are written by Congress, but the taxes are collected by the executive branch.

The judicial branch is the third branch of government. A system of courts makes up the judicial branch. The Supreme Court is the nation's highest court. There are also lower federal courts in every state. The Supreme Court has nine

commander in chief
head of the Army, Navy, Air Force, and Marines

declare war
announce war

Here, President Franklin D. Roosevelt signs a bill.

judges who are chosen by the President. The most important job of the Supreme Court is to decide if the laws passed by Congress are constitutional or unconstitutional. Constitutional laws obey the guidelines of the Constitution; unconstitutional laws do not obey the Constitution. The Supreme Court also decides if actions taken by Congress or the President are constitutional or unconstitutional.

Checks and Balances

Checks and balances were written into the Constitution to prevent any one branch of government from becoming too powerful. The power of government is balanced among the three branches. To keep it balanced, each branch checks the actions of the other branches.

What are some important checks and balances? Congress alone does not pass laws. The President reads every law and then decides whether to sign the law or to **veto** it. If the President vetoes the law, Congress can then vote on this law again. In this way the President checks the power of Congress. The Senate and the House of Representatives can **override** the President's veto if two thirds of the senators and representatives vote for the law. Since 1789, presidents have vetoed more than 2,000 laws. Congress has been able to override those vetoes only about one hundred times. The President's veto checks and balances the power of Congress to make laws. The power of Congress to override vetoes also checks the power of the President.

There are many other checks and balances. The President makes **treaties** with other nations, but Congress must approve them or the treaties cannot be used. The President appoints judges to the Supreme Court and leaders to the Cabinet. The Senate must vote to approve these appointments.

When the Supreme Court finds a law unconstitutional, it is checking and balancing the power of Congress. A President or a Supreme Court judge who commits crimes against the government can be removed from office by Congress. Although Congress has never taken away a President's job, it has removed a number of judges from the Supreme Court.

Checks and balances make democracy work in two ways. First, checks and balances encourage the three branches of government to compromise with each other. The President

veto
turn down

override
vote down

treaties
agreements between nations

compromises by appointing judges who will be approved by the Senate. Congress cooperates by writing laws that will be signed and not vetoed by the President. Congress also compromises by making sure that laws are constitutional.

The second way checks and balances help democracy work is by protecting American freedom. For example, the President can veto laws passed by Congress if the President feels those laws take away the rights of the people. If Congress passes laws that **abuse** the rights of Americans, the Supreme Court can declare those laws unconstitutional, and they will be changed.

abuse
hurt

A Living Constitution

The Framers wrote the Constitution so that it would be a lasting set of guidelines for a changing nation. They wrote the Constitution so that it could change as the nation changed. Article 5 explains how the Constitution can be changed by adding amendments or by changing amendments or articles. Since 1788, there have been 27 amendments added to the Constitution.

The Framers made it difficult to add amendments because they felt the Constitution should be changed only for very important reasons. Thousands of new amendments have been **proposed** in Congress, but only 27 have been added to the

proposed
suggested

The Supreme Court of the United States meets in this building.

Congress sometimes meets to hear the President make a speech.

Constitution in two hundred years. Each new amendment has to receive two thirds of the votes in both the Senate and the House of Representatives. Then three fourths of the states have to ratify the amendments.

The Constitution is often called a living Constitution because it changes to meet the needs of a changing nation. The "elastic clause" in Article 1 is another way the Constitution allows change.

The elastic clause states that Congress can make all laws that are needed to carry out its powers. For example, the Constitution says Congress can pass tax laws. Since 1788, Congress has passed hundreds of tax laws. Congress decides on the ways it needs to spend money, and then it passes tax laws to raise the money it needs. For example, Congress wanted to build highways among the states of the nation. So Congress passed tax laws to raise enough money to build these highways.

When the Framers wrote the Constitution in 1787, the nation had only a few large cities and most Americans were farmers. Today millions of people live and work in large cities across the nation. Separation of powers and checks and balances have helped the government to work well since 1788. The flexibility of the Constitution has allowed it to change as the United States has changed.

Comprehension — *Write the Questions*

Below are the answers for some questions from this chapter. Read each answer. Then write your own question above each answer. Use the question words to help you.

1. What _____ ?

   This paragraph says that justice, liberty, peace, and safety are the goals of the Constitution.

2. Why _____ ?

   They wanted to make sure that the government would not take away the rights of the people.

3. What _____ ?

   This leader appoints Cabinet leaders and Supreme Court judges, carries out the laws of Congress, and is commander in chief.

4. How _____ ?

   Sometimes Congress needs two thirds of the Senate and House of Representatives to approve the law.

5. What _____ ?

   This part of the Constitution allows Congress to write laws to carry out its powers.

6. Why _____ ?

   The President may feel the law is unconstitutional.

Vocabulary — *Exclusions*

One word or phrase in each group below does not belong. Find that word and cross it out. Then write a sentence that tells how the other words are alike.

1. executive   _____
   elastic
   legislative   _____
   judicial
                  _____

2. justice
   liberty
   war
   peace

   _____

   _____

   _____

3. Preamble
   officials
   articles
   amendments

   _____

   _____

   _____

4. declare war
   make taxes
   appoint judges
   approve treaties

   _____

   _____

   _____

Critical Thinking — *Drawing Conclusions*

To draw a **conclusion,** you need to see how information fits together and gives a paragraph meaning. To draw a correct conclusion, you must be sure it is supported by the paragraph.

Read the paragraph below and the sentences that follow it. Put a check in front of the conclusions that can be drawn from the paragraph.

Congress has passed tax laws to raise money to build highways between states. Sometimes the money is used to pay for weapons. Other money is used to pay for the care of state parks. Money is even raised to pay senators and representatives for their work.

_____ 1. Congress passes a lot of tax laws.

_____ 2. Congress needs money for many projects.

_____ 3. The elastic clause helps Congress do its job.

_____ 4. Congress meets in the Capitol.

_____ 5. Money from taxes passed by Congress is used in many ways.

Skill Builder

Reading a Chart

A **chart** lists groups of facts. Charts are used to learn facts quickly. Read the chart below. Then write the answer to each question.

Powers of the Three Branches of Government

 Legislative	 Executive	 Judicial
• Passes laws • Makes taxes • Controls trade between the United States and other nations • Raises an army • Declares war • Prints and coins money	• Carries out laws of Congress • Collects taxes • Sends soldiers into action • Appoints judges to the Supreme Court • Appoints people to the Cabinet • Makes treaties with other nations	• Settles problems between states • Decides if laws are constitutional • Supreme Court can change decision of lower courts • Interprets laws • Decides if President's actions are constitutional

1. What are three powers of the legislative branch?

   _____

2. What are three powers of the executive branch?

   _____

3. What are three powers of the judicial branch?

   _____

4. What do you think are the two most important powers of the legislative branch? Why?

   _____

5. What do you think are the two most important powers of the executive branch? Why?

   _____

6. What do you think are the two most important powers of the judicial branch? Why?

   _____

Chapter 5	# The Bill of Rights and Other Amendments

Consider As You Read
- Why was a Bill of Rights added to the Constitution?
- How do the amendments protect the rights of Americans?

Imagine living in a nation where you might go to jail if you wrote a letter to a newspaper that showed you disagreed with the President of the United States. Try to imagine living in a nation where everyone must pray in the same kind of church each week. What would it be like to live in a nation where you could be sent to jail without a jury trial and be forced to stay in jail because you disagreed with government leaders?

The Framers of the Constitution thought about these problems as they planned the Constitution. They believed that separation of powers, limited government, and checks and balances would prevent the government from taking away the rights of the people.

Adding the Bill of Rights

Many people were unhappy because the Constitution did not have a Bill of Rights. They felt the Constitution did not

The Bill of Rights is on display in Washington, D.C.

guarantee important rights to every American. Many states would not ratify the Constitution because it lacked a Bill of Rights. The Framers did not believe that a Bill of Rights was needed, since most state constitutions already had their own Bill of Rights. The Framers promised to add a Bill of Rights so that the states would ratify the Constitution. With that promise, the Constitution was ratified in 1788. The Bill of Rights was proposed at the first meeting of Congress in 1789. By 1791, the states had ratified these ten important amendments, and they became an important part of the Constitution.

The Bill of Rights did not change the Constitution in any way, but it did make clear which rights the government must protect. These ten amendments tell Americans exactly what their rights are. For example, the Bill of Rights protects freedom of religion, or the right to choose one's religious beliefs. Congress cannot make laws that tell people what religion to follow. It cannot pass laws that require government leaders to belong to religious groups. Such laws would take away the right to freedom of religion.

The Framers had three goals when they wrote the Bill of Rights. First, they wanted to protect the freedom of each person. Second, they wanted to prevent the abuse of power by the government. Third, they wanted to protect people who are accused of crimes. A copy of the Bill of Rights and an explanation of each amendment are at the end of the book. Let's look at some of these amendments closely.

The Five Freedoms of the First Amendment

The First Amendment of the Bill of Rights protects five freedoms. It guarantees freedom of religion to all people in the nation. The separation of church and state, which means that government must be completely separate from religion, is part of the First Amendment. Public schools cannot teach religion. Tax money cannot be used to help religious schools. All citizens and elected leaders can believe in any religion they choose.

The First Amendment also protects freedom of speech and freedom of the press. These two freedoms are important to democracy. These freedoms mean that people can speak or

Many people spoke out against the war in Vietnam.

write against the government. But there are laws that limit these freedoms. It is a crime to shout "Fire!" in a crowded place where there is no fire. Freedom of the press does not allow reporters to write untrue stories about other people.

The First Amendment allows the freedom of peaceful **assembly.** Americans are allowed to gather in groups to show how they feel about a problem. During the 1960s, many people were unhappy that American soldiers were fighting a war in Vietnam. Americans used their right of freedom of assembly to gather together and protest against the war. These protests told the President and Congress how unhappy many Americans were about the war in Vietnam.

Freedom of assembly allows people to join groups that work for causes they agree with. Since the 1960s, many Americans have helped the work of Martin Luther King, Jr., by joining groups that work for **civil rights** laws. Civil rights are the rights given to Americans in the Constitution. Many groups worked hard to win better laws for all Americans. Since 1964, Congress has passed several civil rights laws.

The First Amendment also allows the right to **petition** the government. Americans can call, visit, or write to senators, representatives, and the President about changes they would like to see in the government.

The Fifth and Sixth Amendments

The Fifth Amendment protects people who are accused of crimes in three ways. First, people cannot be forced to speak against themselves. The government must find evidence and prove that the accused person should be sent to jail. The second protection in the Fifth Amendment is the **due process** clause. The due process clause says the government must obey the law and treat accused people fairly. The courts must follow a certain process to decide whether or not a person is **guilty.** The third protection is from **double jeopardy.** Once a jury decides an accused person is not guilty, the accused person cannot be tried for the same crime again in the same court. However, the accused person can ask for another trial in a higher court if due process was not followed.

The Sixth Amendment guarantees every American the right to a fair and speedy jury trial. An accused person cannot be kept in jail for many months waiting for a trial. Since a lawyer

assembly
gathering of people

civil rights
rights belonging to citizens

petition
make requests of

due process
fair treatment

guilty
one who has done wrong

double jeopardy
being tried twice for the same crime

People marched in Washington, D.C., in 1963, to fight for civil rights.

is needed for a fair trial, the government must provide lawyers for people who cannot pay their own lawyers.

Other Important Amendments

Seventeen other amendments have been added to the Constitution since 1791. All amendments and an explanation of their meaning are found at the end of the book. This chapter explains some of the most important amendments.

The Thirteenth, Fourteenth, and Fifteenth amendments were written to help African Americans. They are called the Civil War Amendments since they were added after the Civil War. Before the Civil War, many African Americans were slaves. After the Civil War ended in 1865, the Thirteenth Amendment was added to the Constitution. This amendment ended slavery and prevents the nation from allowing slavery again at any time.

The Fourteenth Amendment of 1868 is an important amendment because it has helped protect civil rights for all Americans. It says that all people who are born or **naturalized** in the United States are citizens.

The Fourteenth Amendment also has an equal protection clause. This means the states must give all people equal protection under the law by treating everyone fairly and equally. At first this amendment was used to help African Americans win civil rights. Now the Fourteenth Amendment is used to help all Americans have equal rights.

naturalized
born in another nation, but made a citizen of the United States

The Fifteenth Amendment was added to the Constitution in 1870. It gave African Americans the right to vote. The government cannot prevent people from voting because of their race or color. However, for almost one hundred years after this amendment was passed, many southern states wrote their own laws to stop certain people from voting. The state laws required citizens to pay poll taxes and pass reading tests in order to vote. The laws prevented many African Americans from voting. The Supreme Court declared some of these laws unconstitutional. Finally, in 1965, Congress passed the Voting Rights Act to end all unfair voting laws. Since 1965, millions of African Americans have used their right to vote.

The Nineteenth Amendment is called the woman **suffrage** amendment because it gave women the right to vote. After this amendment was ratified in 1920, women were allowed to vote in all state and national elections.

The Twenty-second Amendment of 1951 limits the amount of time a person can be President of the United States. George Washington, the first President, served two **terms.** Each term lasted four years. Until 1933, the Presidents after George

suffrage
right to vote

terms
periods of time

In 1870, African Americans were able to vote for the first time.

Many women used their freedoms to fight for the right to vote.

Washington never served more than two terms. Franklin D. Roosevelt became President in 1933 and was elected to four terms. Many Americans thought a President could become too powerful if he served for so many years. So the Twenty-second Amendment was written and ratified. It allows a President to be elected to no more than two terms.

The Twenty-sixth Amendment gave 18-year-olds the right to vote. Before 1971, Americans had to be 21 years old to vote. Soldiers who were 18 years old fought in the army and died in wars for the nation. People felt that if soldiers were old enough to fight and die for the United States, then they were old enough to vote for their President, senators, and representatives.

The Constitution, the Bill of Rights, and the other seventeen amendments have helped the United States become a nation where the rights of the people are protected. It is a nation where the power of government comes from the people. Our Constitution has worked so well it has become a model for other nations. Many nations have used the ideas in our Constitution to plan governments that protect the freedom, liberty, and happiness of their people.

Using What You Learned

Vocabulary — *Match Up*

Choose a word or phrase in the box to complete each sentence. Write that word or phrase on the blank.

due process	terms	assembly	double jeopardy
naturalized	guarantees	petition	suffrage

1. The Bill of Rights _____ the rights of every citizen.

2. Freedom of _____ allows people to gather and share their opinions.

3. In order for accused people to receive fair treatment, the Fifth Amendment has a _____ clause.

4. The Fifth Amendment protects people from _____ so that they cannot be tried twice for the same crime.

5. People are allowed to _____ the government and ask for changes.

6. People who are born or _____ in the United States can vote.

7. The Nineteenth Amendment is for woman _____ .

8. A President can only be elected to two _____ .

Comprehension — *Write the Answer*

Write one or more sentences to answer each question.

1. Why was a Bill of Rights added to the Constitution? _____

_____

2. What freedoms are protected by the First Amendment? _____

_____

3. Why are the freedoms in the First Amendment important for people in a democracy? _____

_____

4. How do the Fifth and Sixth Amendments help accused people? _____

_____

5. Which amendments helped African Americans after the Civil War? _____

_____

6. Why did Americans add the Twenty-sixth Amendment? _____

_____

Critical Thinking — *Distinguishing Relevant Information*

Information that is **relevant** is information that is important for what you want to say or write. Information that is not necessary for what you want to say or write is not relevant.

Imagine that you have to tell a friend how the Bill of Rights protects the rights of citizens. Read each sentence below. Decide which sentences are relevant to what you will say. Put a check in front of the relevant sentences. There are three relevant sentences.

_____ 1. When the Constitution was ratified, the Framers promised that a Bill of Rights would be written.

_____ 2. There are ten amendments in the Bill of Rights.

_____ 3. Some states did not want to ratify the Constitution at first because they wanted to be sure the rights of citizens would be protected.

_____ 4. The Fourth Amendment says that a person's home cannot be searched unless a judge has given permission.

_____ 5. The Sixth Amendment guarantees a person's right to a fair trial.

_____ 6. The Bill of Rights was signed in 1791.

_____ 7. People are allowed to practice any religion, and the Bill of Rights protects this right.

_____ 8. The Bill of Rights is part of the Constitution.

"I have a dream . . ."

In 1963, Martin Luther King, Jr., led a rally of 200,000 people in Washington, D.C. The people at the rally used their First Amendment rights of peaceful assembly and freedom of speech to tell Congress, the President, and millions of Americans that the nation needed a civil rights law. Here is part of the famous speech King gave at that rally.

Martin Luther King, Jr.

Now is the time to make real the promises of Democracy. . . . *Now* is the time to open the doors of opportunity to all of God's children. . . .

1963 is not an end, but a beginning. Those who hope that the Negro needed to blow off steam and will now be content will have a rude awakening if the Nation returns to business as usual. There will be neither rest nor **tranquility** in America until the Negro is granted his citizenship rights. . . .

We can never be satisfied as long as our bodies . . . cannot gain lodging in the motels of the highways and the hotels of the cities. . . . We can never be satisfied as long as a Negro in Mississippi cannot vote and a Negro in New York believes he has nothing for which to vote. . . .

Go back to Mississippi, go back to Alabama . . . knowing that somehow this situation can and will be changed. . . .

I say to you today, my friends, that in spite of the difficulties and **frustrations** of the moment I still have a dream. It is a dream deeply rooted in the American dream. . . .

I have a dream that one day on the red hills of Georgia the sons of former slaves and the sons of former slaveowners will be able to sit down together at the table of brotherhood. . . .

I have a dream that my four little children will one day live in a nation where they will not be judged by the color of their skin but by the content of their character. . . .

This is our hope. This is the faith with which I return to the South. . . . With this faith we will be able to work together, to pray together, to struggle together, to go to jail together, to stand up for freedom together, knowing that we will be free one day.

tranquility
peace

frustrations
feelings of not being satisfied

"Now is the time to make real the promises of Democracy."

This will be the day when all of God's children will be able to sing with new meaning "My country 'tis of thee, sweet land of liberty, of thee I sing. Land where my fathers died, land of the pilgrim's pride, from every mountainside, let freedom ring."

When we let freedom ring . . . from every state and every city, we will be able to speed up that day when all of God's children, black men and white men, Jews and **Gentiles,** Protestants and Catholics, will be able to join hands and sing in the words of the old Negro **spiritual,** "Free at last! Free at last! Thank God almighty, we are free at last!"

Gentiles
non-Jews

spiritual
religious song

The next year, Congress passed the Civil Rights Act of 1964. It has helped millions of Americans win fair and equal treatment.

Write About It

On a separate sheet of paper, write a paragraph that tells in what ways you think King's dream has come true and in what ways it has not.

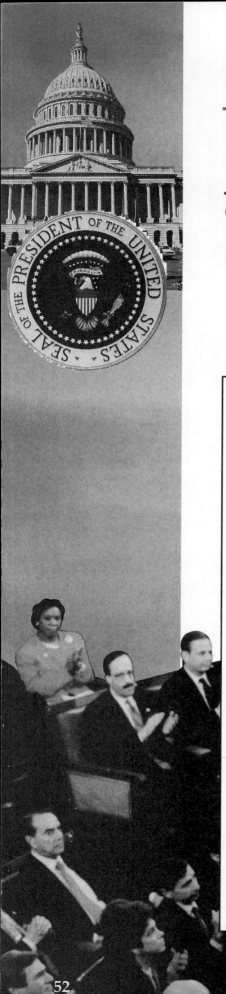

UNIT 2
Three Branches of the Federal Government

The Constitution describes a federal government with three branches. Articles One, Two, and Three explain that separate powers belong to the legislative, the executive, and the judicial branches. By working together, the three branches have been able to govern a growing, changing nation.

The federal government is a government by the American people and for the American people. Members of Congress and the President are elected by the people, and together with the judicial branch, they work for the people. There are few requirements to be a member of Congress, or even to be the President of the United States. Americans of all races and religions, both men and women, can enter elections to serve in the government of the United States.

About three and one-half million people work for the federal government. It is a huge government with more workers than the population of some small nations. Federal government workers do many kinds of jobs in every state. All of these workers have promised to obey the Constitution.

Have You Ever Wondered . . .

- Senators can make speeches of any length. Why would a senator choose to speak for 24 hours?

- The executive branch is the largest branch. Why does the President need so many people working with him?

- The judges on the Supreme Court are not elected. How are Supreme Court judges chosen?

- Three and one-half million people work in the government. What do all those federal workers do?

- The President can veto any bill sent to him by Congress. Why doesn't the President veto bills more often?

The answers to these questions are in this unit. You will learn how each branch uses its constitutional powers and how laws are created for the nation. As you read, think about the ways the federal government meets the needs of a changing nation.

Chapter 6

Congress: The Lawmaking Branch

Consider As You Read
- What are some similarities and differences between the Senate and the House of Representatives?
- How does Congress get its work done?
- How is Congress the voice of the American people?

A new term of Congress begins on January third of every odd-numbered year. On that day, all new members of Congress stand and take an **oath,** promising to obey the Constitution. A new term of Congress has begun. During that term, members will spend most of their time writing laws for the nation.

oath
promise

The Powers of Congress

The main responsibility of Congress is to make laws for the United States, but Congress also has other powers. Article 1, the longest article in the Constitution, explains eight powers

The Senate and the House of Representatives meet in the Capitol.

of Congress. The chart below explains the powers of Congress. Congress can also propose amendments to the Constitution and allow new states to become part of the United States.

The powers of Congress are also limited. It can do only what the Constitution says are its jobs. There are many things Congress cannot do. Congress cannot make laws to create a national school system. It cannot pass laws that abuse the rights of Americans. Only the state governments have the power to pass laws about marriage, divorce, school rules, and drivers' licenses.

POWERS OF CONGRESS

	Power	How Congress Uses Its Power
1.	make taxes	Congress decides how the nation should spend money. Congress uses tax money to pay for highways between states, free school lunches, space programs, national parks, science research, and many other projects.
2.	borrow money	Congress borrows money by selling government bonds and certificates.
3.	establish courts	Congress sets up all federal courts that are below the Supreme Court.
4.	coin money	Congress makes laws for the printing and coining of all United States money.
5.	war powers	Congress can declare war and has done so five times since 1787. Congress supports the Army, Navy, Air Force, and Marines.
6.	commerce	Congress controls business between states and with foreign nations. Congress can pass laws to control all transportation, business, and television programs between states.
7.	foreign relations	Congress approves or disapproves treaties that the President signs with other nations.
8.	other powers	Congress creates post offices and makes rules for the post offices. Congress passes laws about citizenship and **immigration.** Congress controls **copyrights** and **patents.**

immigration
people moving from one nation to another

copyrights
the rights to publish written work

patents
the right to make, use, and sell something that a person has invented

The Job of Congress

The Framers of the Constitution organized Congress into two houses, the Senate and the House of Representatives. Together these two houses make up the lawmaking branch of the government.

The most important job of Congress is to make laws for the nation. Most lawmaking work is done by groups of people in **committee.** Congress needs committees because all members do not have time to study each of the thousands of new bills that are proposed during each session. The members of each committee are familiar with the topics of the bills they read. They want to be sure that the bills will do what Congress wants them to do.

There are many committees in both houses of Congress. Committees study bills dealing with different types of problems such as trade, taxes, education, and banking. Some committees that have more power than others are called major committees. Every senator and representative must serve on at least one committee, and each wants to serve on major committees. Often, only those members who have served many terms in Congress are appointed to major committees. Newer members are appointed to committees that are less important.

Committees study the many bills that are sent to them during each session. Committee members also study the problems the new bills try to solve. Committee members try to learn how the people of their districts and states feel about the problems and the proposed bills. If the members feel the bill is important, they will send the bill back to the House or Senate so members can vote on that bill. Sometimes the committee changes the bill before they send it back to the House or Senate. Many bills never make it back. The members decide that the bill is not important enough, and they let it die. Chapter 10 explains how a proposed bill becomes a law.

The Members of Congress

There are one hundred senators—two senators from each state. Senators serve six-year terms and can be reelected. The House of Representatives, with 435 members, is much larger than the Senate. The number of representatives from a state depends on that state's population. States gain or lose

committee
group of people who work together on a certain job

This Representative traveled to Africa for his committee.

56

This shows the Senate chamber in 1934.

representatives as their population becomes larger or smaller. The six states with the smallest population send only one representative to the House. California, the nation's most populated state, has 52 representatives. Members of the House of Representatives serve two-year terms, and they are often reelected many times. There is no limit to how many times a senator or representative can be reelected.

The Constitution describes certain requirements for people to become members of Congress. To be a representative, a person must be at least 25 years old, and he or she must have been a United States citizen for seven years. Senators must have been American citizens for nine years, and they must be at least thirty years old. Both senators and representatives must live in the state that they represent. Members of the House usually live in the districts that they represent.

Members of Congress have many things in common that are not explained in the Constitution. Most members of Congress are middle-aged white men who have graduated from college. Many members are lawyers. Most members are married and have children. Members in the House of Representatives of the 104th Congress include 47 women, 38 African Americans, 17 Hispanics, and 4 Asian Americans. Only eight women are United States Senators. There are two Asian Americans, one African American, and one Native American in the Senate.

Every member of Congress belongs to a **political party.** The Republicans and the Democrats are our nation's largest political parties. Political parties are important in Congress. Members of Congress often vote for laws that put the ideas of

political party
group of people who work together to put their ideas into action

their party into action. The party with the most members in Congress is called the majority party. The minority party has fewer members in Congress.

Every member of the House of Representatives represents about the same number of people. States that send more than one representative to the House are divided into congressional districts. Each district has equal representation in Congress. In order to give the people of different racial groups fair representation in Congress, districts are sometimes formed to keep the people in these groups together. In this way the representative can best work for the people of his or her district.

A **census** is taken every ten years to count the number of people in each district. District lines are changed when a census shows that the population in a district has grown larger or smaller. The district lines are redrawn so that each district in the nation will have about the same population.

Leadership in Congress

The Speaker of the House is the leader of the House of Representatives. At the start of each new term, members of the House elect the Speaker of the House. The Speaker of the House is a powerful leader who controls all sessions of the House of Representatives. No representative can speak without permission from the Speaker of the House. The Speaker appoints people to work on different committees and signs bills that are passed by the House.

President Roosevelt spoke to the House of Representatives in 1935.

The Constitution appoints the Vice President as president of the Senate. The Vice President has little power in the Senate. He cannot speak about proposed bills, and he can vote only to break a tie vote. Since the Vice President is often unable to lead Senate meetings because of other responsibilities, the Senate elects a temporary president called the president *pro tempore* to lead meetings when the Vice President is away.

pro tempore
Latin meaning "for the time"

The most powerful leaders in the Senate are the majority and minority party leaders. These two senators plan how decisions will be made in their party. They also appoint members to committees.

How Congress Gets Work Done

Senators and representatives meet to develop new laws during each two-year term of Congress. Each term has two regular sessions that last for many months of the year. The members of Congress try to prepare all new laws for the nation during these regular sessions. A session of Congress **adjourns** when both the House and Senate agree that they have finished their work for the year.

adjourns
ends

After Congress adjourns, the President of the United States can call on Congress to meet in a special session before the next regular session begins in January. Presidents call special sessions when there are serious problems that cannot wait until the regular session begins. Presidents do not call many special sessions of Congress. Special sessions are saved for extremely important business.

The Voice of the People

Congress is the voice of the American people because all of its members are elected by the voters of every state. Congress passes hundreds of new laws each year. Sometimes members of Congress have to pass laws that they know their voters won't like because they believe the nation needs these laws. For example, few Americans want to pay higher taxes, but in 1990, Congress passed laws that raised taxes for millions of people. The government needed more money to pay for its many projects and its large debt. Since 1789, the members of Congress have written thousands of laws that have helped both their states and the American nation.

Speaker of the House Newt Gingrich

Vocabulary — *Match Up*

Choose a word or phrase from the box to complete each sentence. Write that word or phrase on the blank.

term	**bills**	**president** *pro tempore*	
census	**oath**	**political party**	**adjourns**

1. Members of Congress take an _____ and promise to obey the Constitution.

2. District lines are often changed after a _____ has been taken.

3. Committees meet to discuss proposed _____ .

4. Members of Congress usually vote in the way their _____ would want them to.

5. When Congress finishes its work, it _____ .

6. One _____ of Congress lasts two years.

7. The temporary president of the Senate is the _____ .

Comprehension — *Write the Answer*

Write one or more sentences to answer each question.

1. What are the requirements in the Constitution for becoming a senator? _____

_____

2. Why are some districts redrawn after a census? _____

_____

3. What are three things that a committee can do with a bill? _____

_____

_____

4. Why does Congress sometimes pass laws that many Americans dislike? _____

_____

5. What are two ways that members of Congress are a voice of the people? _____

_____

_____

6. What are three powers of Congress that you think are most important? Why? _____

_____

_____

_____

Critical Thinking — *Analogies*

Use a word or phrase in the box to finish each sentence. You will not use all the words.

minority party	**districts**	**Speaker of the House**	**minor**
senators	**Congress**	**judges**	**commerce**

1. Senators are to states as representatives are to _____ .

2. Two-year terms are to representatives as six-year terms are to

   _____ .

3. The Vice President is to the Senate as the _____ is to the
   House of Representatives.

4. The majority party is to most members of Congress as the _____
   is to fewer members of Congress.

5. Declaring war is to war powers as controlling business with foreign nations

   is to _____ .

Chapter 7

The President and the Executive Branch

Consider As You Read
- What are the powers and jobs of the President?
- How do Congress and the Supreme Court check and balance the President's power?

execute
carry out

In 1789, George Washington placed one hand on a Bible as he stood before a large crowd and stated this oath from the Constitution: "I do solemnly swear (or affirm) that I will faithfully **execute** the office of the President of the United States, and will to the best of my ability, preserve, protect, and defend the Constitution of the United States." With that oath, Washington became the nation's first President. Every President since then has started his term in office by repeating that same oath.

President Reagan took the oath of office in 1981.

George Bush and Dan Quayle made a speech at the 1988 Republican Party National Convention.

Planning the Executive Branch

The Framers of the Constitution created the executive branch to carry out all laws written by Congress. They decided that the leader of the executive branch would be the nation's leader. The Framers created a new type of job, the **presidency.** For the first time in history an elected leader with limited power would rule a large nation.

presidency
job of the President

The Constitution states only a few requirements for becoming President of the United States. A person must be born in the United States, have lived here for at least fourteen years, and be at least 35 years old. Millions of Americans meet these requirements.

Americans often elect Presidents who have the right **image.** The President should be a strong leader who will be an example of fine behavior for the entire nation. Voters want the President to be a good speaker who is friendly, smart, and likable. Most Presidents have experience as state governors or as members of Congress before becoming the nation's leader. Most Presidents have been married men with families. So far, all 42 Presidents have been white, Christian men. However, the Constitution allows men and women from all races and religions to become the nation's President.

image
character; personality

The Framers wanted the President to be paid a salary. Congress decides the amount of that salary, which is now $200,000 a year. The President has a home in the White House while he is in office. In addition, the President can use the cars, planes, and helicopters that belong to the executive branch.

The Role of the Vice President

The Constitution also created the job of Vice President. There are no requirements to be Vice President. The Constitution gives the Vice President only two powers. The first power is to be president of the Senate. The second power is to act as president when the President is unable for any reason to do the job.

responsibilities
duties; jobs

During the past forty years, Vice Presidents have been given more **responsibilities.** As Vice President, George Bush was given many responsibilities by President Ronald Reagan. Bush had his own office in the White House, attended Cabinet meetings, and met with President Reagan every week. President Reagan appointed Bush to serve as the chairperson of several important **agencies.** When President Reagan was

agencies
offices for certain jobs

When President Kennedy was shot in 1963, his Vice President, Lyndon Baines Johnson, took the oath of office and became the next President.

Vice President Al Gore and President Bill Clinton discuss an issue.

unable to work, Bush acted as President until Reagan was able to do the job. Bush became President of the United States in 1988. His experience as Vice President helped prepare him for the responsibilities of the presidency. Unlike George Bush, most Vice Presidents do not win election to the presidency. Only nine Vice Presidents have been elected President of the United States.

Article 2 and the Twenty-fifth Amendment explain that the Vice President would have the job of president if the President dies while in office. This prevents the nation from being without a President for even one day. It is important for the nation to always have a leader. On November 22, 1963, President John F. Kennedy was shot and killed. In less than two hours, Vice President Johnson became the nation's new President. In the history of the nation, eight Presidents have died while in office, and their Vice Presidents immediately became President.

The Powers of the President

The Constitution describes the powers of the presidency in Article 2. The President uses these powers to do six major jobs.

Chief Executive. The President leads the executive branch in carrying out the laws of Congress. As Chief Executive, the President helps plan the nation's **budget** and appoints leaders

budget
plan for spending money

65

to the Cabinet. These Cabinet leaders plan programs to carry out the laws of Congress.

Commander in Chief. The President is the leader of two million members of the armed forces. The President can send troops into action anywhere in the world for sixty days without the approval of Congress.

Chief Diplomat. In this role the President appoints ambassadors to other nations and makes treaties with foreign nations. The President plans the foreign **policies** of the United States.

policies
plans of action

Chief Lawmaker. Once a year the President delivers a "State of the Union" speech to Congress. This speech explains the President's goals and plans for the nation, and it sometimes tells Congress what laws are needed to meet these goals. The President suggests bills to Congress at other times as well. The President must read all bills passed by Congress. A bill only becomes a law when it is signed by the President. Sometimes Presidents use their veto power to stop bills from becoming laws.

Chief of State. As **Chief of State,** he is a **symbol** of the nation. He attends ceremonies, gives out awards, and greets the leaders of foreign nations.

Chief of State
person who represents the whole nation

symbol
something that stands for something else

The Joint Chiefs of Staff advise the President on issues of security.

During Watergate, members of the Senate and House looked into the actions of some Republican Party members.

Party Chief. The President leads his political party. He works to put his party's ideas into action. The President often works for other party members to help them win elections.

The Constitution also limits the power of the President through the system of checks and balances. The Senate must approve all of the President's appointments to the Supreme Court and the Cabinet. The Senate must approve foreign treaties and the appointment of **ambassadors** to foreign nations. With enough votes, Congress can override the President's veto and pass a law that the President **opposes.** The Supreme Court can declare the President's actions unconstitutional, and the President must correct his actions. Congress can **impeach** a President who has committed crimes or acted wrongly. If the President is found guilty, he will be removed from office. This has never happened in the nation's history.

ambassadors
representatives of one nation in another nation

opposes
goes against

impeach
charge with committing crimes or acting wrongly

President Nixon and the Watergate Scandal

An event called the Watergate Scandal is a good example of how checks and balances limit the President's power. In 1972, Richard Nixon, a Republican, was President and wanted to win reelection. In that year, a group of people who were working for Nixon's reelection decided to steal the campaign

Richard M. Nixon

plans of the Democrats. They broke into the offices of the Democrats in the Watergate building in Washington, D.C. Months later, newspaper reporters showed that members of the President's staff knew about the Watergate break-in.

Congress wanted to know what really happened at Watergate. The members of Congress wanted to know if President Nixon and his staff were guilty of crimes against the federal government. The Senate formed a committee to learn more about the Watergate events. The committee members believed that tapes Nixon made of conversations in his office would provide information about the events. The Supreme Court ordered President Nixon to give his tapes to Congress.

At first Nixon refused, but the Supreme Court said a President cannot use his power to "cover up" crimes, and Nixon was forced to turn over his tapes. A special committee in the House of Representatives listened to the tapes and decided that Nixon had committed crimes and should be impeached. Nixon resigned from the presidency because he did not want to go on trial before the Senate. The Vice President, Gerald Ford, became the next President on the same day that Nixon resigned. A few weeks later, President Ford **pardoned** Nixon of any crimes he might have committed. Many members of Nixon's staff went to jail because of their Watergate crimes.

pardoned
excused

The Executive Bureaucracy

The President alone cannot carry out the many responsibilities of the executive branch. Fourteen Cabinet departments advise the President and share responsibilities with him. Many agencies and **bureaus** are part of the executive branch and help carry out the laws of Congress. These agencies and bureaus form a huge executive **bureaucracy.** More than three million people work in this bureaucracy. Chapter 8 explains how the Cabinet and the agencies execute the laws of Congress. The President, the Cabinet, and all members of the executive bureaucracy share the responsibilities of carrying out the many laws of Congress.

bureaus
groups of people with a certain job

bureaucracy
many groups of people doing many jobs

Using What You Learned

Comprehension — *Write a Paragraph*

Use eight or more words or phrases below to write a paragraph that describes three ways that the President carries out the job of leader of the nation.

foreign policies	responsibilities	chief executive
"State of the Union"	commander in chief	appoint
agencies	diplomat	treaties
budget	veto	political party
laws		

_____

_____

_____

_____

_____

_____

_____

Vocabulary — *Find the Meaning*

Write on the blank the word or phrase that best completes each sentence.

1. An **ambassador** is a representative in a _____ .

    court   foreign nation   Congress

2. As **Chief of State,** the President is a _____ of the nation.

    diplomat   symbol   lawmaker

3. A **budget** is a plan for _____ .

    spending money   making taxes   writing laws

4. When the President plans **foreign policy,** he decides how the United States will

   _____ .

        pardon crimes   give awards   deal with other nations

5. Congress may decide to **impeach** a President because the President

   _____ .

        committed a crime   vetoed a bill   spent too much money

6. Many **agencies** and **bureaus** form the _____ .

        Senate   legislative branch   bureaucracy

Critical Thinking — *Categories*

   Read the words in each group. Decide how they are alike. Write a title for each group on the blank beside each group. You may use the words in the box for all or part of each title.

executive lawmaker	diplomat state	commander chief

1. leader of Army
   leader of Navy
   sends troops into action

   _____

2. leads executive branch
   carries out laws
   appoints Cabinet leaders

   _____

3. symbol of United States
   attends ceremonies
   greets foreign visitors

   _____

4. appoints ambassadors
   makes treaties
   plans foreign policy

   _____

5. signs bills into law
   vetoes bills
   State of the Union speech to Congress

   _____

Skill Builder

Understanding Political Cartoons

Political cartoons use pictures to express an opinion about a political situation. Sometimes cartoons may seem funny, but they are usually about serious ideas. The cartoon below is about President Nixon and Watergate. The painting in the cartoon is of the signing of the Constitution. Look at the cartoon. Then write the answer to each question.

"Hey guys, do you really think we need that clause about impeachment in there?"

1. Why did Congress want to impeach Nixon? _____

   _____

2. What executive powers did Congress think Nixon had abused? _____

   _____

3. Why do you think the cartoonist showed Nixon at the signing of the Constitution?

   _____

4. What could Nixon have done to the Constitution to keep Congress from wanting to

   impeach him? _____

   _____

5. Write two sentences that explain what the cartoonist thinks about Nixon and the

   Watergate scandal. _____

   _____

   _____

Barbara Jordan (1936–1996)

Barbara Jordan

When Barbara Jordan was in high school, she and her friends could only eat in certain restaurants. The Supreme Court had not yet ruled on *Brown v. Topeka Board of Education*. There was still segregation in Texas. Jordan knew that this was wrong. She also knew that to work for change all over she should work for change in her own neighborhood. So Barbara Jordan decided to become a lawyer.

Jordan went to law school in Boston. There were few women lawyers, and even fewer African American women lawyers. Jordan knew that the education she got in Texas was not equal to that of the white students at the law school. So she worked hard to prove that she could be a good lawyer.

When Jordan returned to Texas, she set up her law office in her parents' dining room. But she began to feel that she could not help people in the way she wanted. So Jordan ran for the office of state representative. She ran and lost in 1962 and again in 1964, but she was determined. So she ran for the state senate in 1966. This time she won. She was the first African American elected to the Texas State Senate since 1888.

In 1972, Jordan became the first African American woman from the South to be elected to the United States House of Representatives. She was reelected twice to Congress. Many people thought that she could be Vice President, or even President, but Jordan liked her job as representative.

Barbara Jordan was well-known for her great speaking ability.

Chapter 8

The Executive Branch at Work

Consider As You Read

- What do the three parts of the executive bureaucracy do?
- How do some of the departments and agencies carry out the laws of Congress?
- How can the executive branch change to meet the needs of a changing nation?

Every day people in the United States mail millions of letters. More than 30,000 post offices and 800,000 workers are part of the United States Postal Service. It is just one of the hundreds of agencies in the huge executive bureaucracy.

Organization of the Executive Branch

The President of the United States leads the nation's largest branch of government, the executive branch. This branch is divided into three parts: the Executive Office of the President, the executive departments, and about two hundred independent agencies. About three million workers in offices in all fifty states are part of the executive bureaucracy. They do thousands of different jobs to carry out the laws of Congress.

Delivering the mail is just one job of the executive branch.

The Executive Office of the President has fewer staff members than the two other parts of the executive bureaucracy. The President lives and works in the White House. The White House staff and several important councils form the Executive Office of the President. The White House staff has about four hundred members who work closely with the President and help him handle his daily business. Most staff members have their offices in the White House. The White House staff includes advisers, lawyers, and speech writers. The President's Chief of Staff controls and organizes the White House staff.

Besides the White House staff, the Executive Office includes several agencies. These agencies advise the President on how to enforce the laws of Congress. The National Security Council and the Office of Management and Budget are two agencies in the Executive Office. The National Security Council helps the President plan policies for foreign affairs and **national security.** The Office of Management and Budget helps the President plan the **annual** budget for the nation. This budget is a spending plan for using tax money to meet the President's goals.

national security
keeping the nation safe

annual
yearly

The President works in the Oval Office.

President Bill Clinton meets with members of the Cabinet.

The Executive Departments

The fourteen executive departments form the largest part of the executive branch. They are responsible for carrying out the laws of Congress. For example, labor laws are carried out by the Department of Labor. Laws about airplane transportation are enforced by the Department of Transportation. The President appoints the **secretary** of each department. The secretaries usually belong to the same political party as the President. They must be approved by the Senate.

secretary
leader

The President's Cabinet is made up of the secretaries of the fourteen executive departments. The President cannot be an expert in every area in which he must make decisions. So the Cabinet members advise him on the thousands of serious decisions he makes. Each President decides just how much help he needs from the Cabinet. Some Presidents have many meetings with their Cabinet members, while others depend on their Executive Office staff for most advice.

Some executive departments have many agencies. Two million people in offices throughout our nation work in these agencies. The chart on pages 76–79 provides information about each of the fourteen executive departments and some of their important agencies. Let's take a closer look at three executive departments.

EXECUTIVE DEPARTMENTS AND MAJOR AGENCIES

Departments/Leaders	Major Agencies
Department of Agriculture Secretary of Agriculture	Food Safety and Inspection Service Food and Nutrition Service Commodity Credit Corporation
Department of Commerce Secretary of Commerce	International Trade Administration Bureau of Census Patent and Trademark Office National Weather Service
Department of Defense Secretary of Defense	Joint Chiefs of Staff Department of the Army Department of the Navy Department of the Air Force

Department of Education
Secretary of Education
	Assistant Secretary for Elementary
	  and Secondary Education
	Assistant Secretary for Educational
	  Research and Improvement

Department of Energy Secretary of Energy	Assistant Secretary for Conservation and Renewable Energy Assistant Secretary for Nuclear Energy

Department of Health and
  Human Services
Secretary of Health and
  Human Services
	Social Security Administration
	Food and Drug Administration (F.D.A.)
	Public Health Service

Department of Housing and
  Urban Development
Secretary of Housing and
  Urban Development
	Assistant Secretary for Housing
	Assistant Secretary for Public and
	  Indian Housing

inspects
looks at very closely

low income
those who earn a
small amount

coining
making

Millions of Americans benefit from the Department of Agriculture because it **inspects** our meat, poultry, and dairy products. If foods are healthy and safe to eat, the inspector stamps them with "U.S.D.A." to show the buyer that the foods are safe. This department also provides much of the food needed for school lunch programs across the nation. It provides food stamps to help **low income** families buy food.

The Department of the Treasury carries out the jobs of **coining** money and collecting taxes. This department was started by George Washington more than two hundred years ago. Two agencies within the department print all paper

Department Responsibilities

Inspects and grades dairy products, meat, and poultry
Controls school lunch and food stamp program
Helps farmers

Promotes trade with other nations
Carries out a census every ten years
Issues patents
Promotes economic growth

Maintains armed forces
Advises the President on security and military affairs
Builds military bases

Studies problems in education
Provides money for many school programs
Advises the President about education programs

Finds sources of energy
Protects the energy supply
Controls the use of nuclear energy

Controls Social Security and Medicare programs
Checks and approves the safety of new medicines
Controls health and welfare programs

Helps state and local governments with urban problems
Helps provide better housing for people with low incomes

money and produce all coins. Another agency, the Internal Revenue Service, with offices in every state, collects federal tax money. The Secret Service is another agency within the Department of the Treasury. In 1865, Congress created this agency to stop the production of **counterfeit** money. After President McKinley was shot and killed in 1901, the Secret Service began to protect Presidents. Today the Secret Service also protects the Vice President, the families of the Presidents and Vice President, and visiting leaders from other nations.

The Department of Justice provides legal advice to the President. It represents the United States in federal court

counterfeit
fake

EXECUTIVE DEPARTMENTS AND MAJOR AGENCIES

Departments/Leaders	Major Agencies
Department of the Interior Secretary of the Interior	United States Fish and Wildlife Service Bureau of Indian Affairs
Department of Justice Attorney General	Immigration and Naturalization Service (I.N.S.) Civil Rights Division Federal Bureau of Investigation (F.B.I.) Bureau of Prisons
Department of Labor Secretary of Labor	Employment and Training Administration Pension and Welfare Benefits Association Bureau of Labor Statistics
Department of State Secretary of State	Bureau for Refugee Programs Bureau of African Affairs Bureau of Consular Affairs
Department of Transportation Secretary of Transportation	United States Coast Guard Federal Aviation Administration Federal Highway Administration
Department of the Treasury Secretary of the Treasury	U.S. Mint U.S. Secret Service Internal Revenue Service (I.R.S.) U.S. Customs Service Bureau of Engraving

Department of Veteran
   Affairs
Secretary of Veteran Affairs
	Veterans Health Services and Research
	   Administration
	Veterans Benefits Administration

cases. Those law cases that involve civil rights laws are handled by the agency called the Civil Rights Division. The Federal Bureau of Investigation (F.B.I.) finds evidence for government court cases to prove whether people are guilty of crimes. Without evidence, a person cannot be found guilty and punished. The Immigration and Naturalization Service (I.N.S.) carries out the citizenship and immigration laws of Congress. This agency helps immigrants become citizens, and it tries to stop **undocumented** workers from entering the nation.

undocumented
without papers showing
you are a U.S. citizen

Department Responsibilities
Protects fish, wildlife, and natural resources Takes care of federal lands and national parks Controls Native American reservations
Provides legal advice to the President Represents the United States in Court Manages federal prisons
Enforces laws on minimum wage and job discrimination Manages unemployment and job training programs Publishes information about salaries, prices, and employment
Helps the President plan and carry out foreign policy Maintains embassies with ambassadors in foreign nations Represents the United States at the United Nations
Enforces safety laws for air, sea, and land transportation Manages interstate highways and railroads Helps cities and states run bus and train systems
Coins money Provides secret service officers Collects federal tax money and customs duties on imported goods
Provides medical and financial help to people who have served in the armed forces

The Independent Agencies

Independent agencies are the third part of the executive bureaucracy. There are now about two hundred independent agencies, with more than one million workers. These agencies are independent of the fourteen executive departments, but they are not independent of the executive branch. Their leaders are appointed by the President, with approval by the Senate. These agencies have many different goals and purposes. The chart on page 80 lists twelve of these agencies and their responsibilities.

A Space Shuttle

NASA, one of the largest independent agencies, controls the nation's space program. Congress formed this agency in 1958. NASA sent astronauts to the moon when the *Apollo 11* spaceship landed on the moon in 1969. Since then, NASA has sent many different kinds of spaceships to faraway planets and for trips around Earth. NASA's research has helped the United States produce better computers, better weapons for defense, and new kinds of medicine.

Civil Service and the Executive Branch

The President appoints people to be leaders of the executive departments, independent agencies, and members of the Executive Office staff. Most people appointed by a President

INDEPENDENT AGENCIES	
Agency	**Responsibility**
Central Intelligence Agency (C.I.A.)	Collects information about other nations
Commission on Civil Rights	Enforces civil rights laws
Consumer Product Safety Commission (C.P.S.C.)	Works to promote safety through research and safety laws
Environmental Protection Agency (E.P.A.)	Enforces laws to protect the nation's air, land, and water
Equal Employment Opportunity Commission (E.E.O.C.)	Carries out laws to prevent job discrimination
Federal Communications Commission (F.C.C.)	Controls all TV and radio stations and telephone service between states
Federal Deposit Insurance Corporation (F.D.I.C.)	Provides insurance on many kinds of bank deposits
Federal Election Commission	Carries out laws on federal elections
Interstate Commerce Commission (I.C.C.)	Controls transportation between states
National Railroad Passenger Corporation (AMTRAK)	Controls railroad service between states
Peace Corps	Sends volunteers to developing nations
Small Business Administration (S.B.A.)	Provides help to small businesses

These people working at the FBI are part of the executive branch.

must find new jobs when the President's term ends. The next President appoints hundreds of new people, mostly from his own political party, to be leaders in the executive bureaucracy. But most of the three million executive branch workers are not hired by a President. Most of them are **civil service** workers who are hired by the Office of Personnel Management, an independent executive branch agency. These civil service workers are hired for federal jobs in every state. They can belong to any political party. Civil service workers cannot be fired when a President's administration ends. They often work for the government until they are ready to retire.

civil service
jobs in the government

A Changing and Growing Branch of Government

The executive branch is always changing to meet the needs of the nation. In 1789, there were only four executive departments. Now there are fourteen, plus hundreds of executive agencies. The executive branch also changes by removing agencies it no longer needs and by creating other departments and agencies to carry out new laws.

The nation spends billions of dollars paying salaries to more than three million executive branch workers. Does the nation really need all of these workers, departments, and agencies? Many people think the executive bureaucracy has become too big. They believe that agencies in the executive departments do the same work as many independent agencies do. They feel these agencies should be cut. Perhaps one day many independent agencies will be closed. Until then a large executive branch will continue to carry out the hundreds of new laws Congress passes each year.

Comprehension — *Write the Questions*

Below are the answers for some questions from this chapter. Read each answer. Then write your own question above each answer. Use the question words to help you.

1. What _____ ?

    These two agencies are part of the Executive Office of the President and plan policies for foreign affairs and the budget.

2. What _____ ?

    This executive department controls school lunch programs and food stamps to low income families.

3. What _____ ?

    This agency, as part of the Department of Justice, carries out laws to help people enter the nation and become citizens.

4. What _____ ?

    These workers are hired by the Office of Personnel Management and can belong to any political party.

Vocabulary — *Exclusions*

One word or phrase in each group below does not belong. Find that word or phrase and cross it out. Then write a sentence that tells how the other words are alike.

1. Peace Corps
   E.P.A.
   Department of Defense
   C.I.A.

   _____

   _____

   _____

2. Executive Office
   Congress
   executive departments
   independent agencies

   _____

   _____

   _____

3. foreign policy
   stop counterfeit money
   collect taxes
   protect President

   _____

   _____

   _____

4. computers
   food stamps
   medicine
   Apollo 11

   _____

   _____

   _____

Critical Thinking — *Fact or Opinion*

Read each sentence below. If the sentence is a fact, write **F** on the blank. If the sentence is an opinion, write **O** on the blank. If the sentence gives both a fact and an opinion, write **FO** on the blank and circle the part of the sentence that is an opinion.

_____ 1. The National Security Council and the Office of Management and Budget are part of the Executive Office of the President.

_____ 2. It is not necessary for the Department of Agriculture to inspect meat and dairy products.

_____ 3. The Department of the Interior can do the work of the Environmental Protection Agency.

_____ 4. The Secret Service protects the President, Vice President, and their families— the most important job in the executive branch.

_____ 5. The Federal Bureau of Investigation finds evidence to prove whether people are guilty of crimes.

_____ 6. There are about two hundred independent agencies whose work should be done by executive departments.

_____ 7. The Department of Health and Human Services helps older Americans by sending social security checks to them.

_____ 8. To do a good job, civil service workers should belong to the President's political party.

Chapter 9

Justice for All: The Judicial Branch

Consider As You Read

- What kinds of federal courts did Congress establish?
- What kinds of decisions does the Supreme Court make, and how do they affect the nation?
- What is judicial review, and why is it important?

"Equal justice under law" are the words written on the front of the United States Supreme Court building. These words remind Americans that the aim of the judicial branch is to work for justice in the nation. Justice means the fair treatment of every person. One goal of the Constitution is "to establish justice." Justice is the right of every American. Although the judicial branch has fewer workers than the other branches, this branch makes important decisions that have a long-lasting effect on the nation.

The Supreme Court building is in Washington, D.C.

The Supreme Court is the highest court in the nation.

The Federal Court System

The Constitution established only one court for the nation, the Supreme Court. It gave Congress the power to establish lower federal courts. It also allowed the states to create their own court systems. Since 1789, Congress has created several different kinds of federal courts.

The first Congress created District Courts for the nation. There is at least one District Court in each state. District Courts are trial courts in which juries hear evidence about crimes against the federal government.

The nation also has eleven Courts of Appeal. These courts were established by Congress in 1891 to decide whether or not the decisions made by District Courts followed due process. Decisions made here are final unless the case is **appealed** to the Supreme Court, which rarely happens.

The Supreme Court is the highest court in the nation. The Supreme Court can **overturn** decisions made by lower courts. Decisions made by the Supreme Court are final; they cannot be appealed to another court.

Federal judges are always appointed by the President of the United States, with approval by the Senate. The President usually appoints judges who belong to his political party and

appealed
sent to a higher court for another decision

overturn
change; reverse

share many of his ideas. Judges in District Courts, Courts of Appeal, and the Supreme Court are allowed to serve lifetime terms. Since judges do not have to think about being elected to office, they can make decisions without worrying whether they will please or anger the voters.

The Constitution does not list requirements for becoming a federal judge, but most of these judges are lawyers. Many have served in their state courts and in Congress. The President tries to appoint people who are able to interpret the law and make fair decisions.

The Supreme Court at Work

Nine judges decide the cases of the United States Supreme Court. Supreme Court judges are called justices. The head of the Supreme Court is called the Chief Justice. Supreme Court justices meet from October through June. During that time, about 4,500 cases are appealed to the Supreme Court. However, the justices have time to hear only about two hundred of them. They try to choose the most important cases that require decisions based on the Constitution.

The Supreme Court justices study each case and then vote on a decision. A majority vote is needed for a decision. Then

The Senate must approve appointments to the Supreme Court. Here members of the Senate question a man whom President Reagan suggested.

Due process is followed during trials.

the justices publish written opinions about the case that explain why the decision was made. These decisions establish **precedents** for judging future court cases.

Justices make four different kinds of decisions on cases that are brought to the Supreme Court. First, justices decide whether the laws of Congress are constitutional. Second, the Supreme Court can decide if state laws are constitutional. Third, the Court can decide if a President's actions, such as Nixon's actions about Watergate, are constitutional. Fourth, the Court can decide on how to settle problems between two states. For example, in 1962 the Supreme Court decided that it was unconstitutional to require students to say certain prayers in public schools. This decision was based on the separation of church and state described in the First Amendment. The 1962 Supreme Court decision explained how to apply the First Amendment to the nation's public schools.

precedents
guidelines

The Importance of Judicial Review

Judicial review is one of the Supreme Court's most important powers. Judicial review allows the Supreme Court to overturn any law that it decides is unconstitutional. The Supreme Court can overturn acts of the executive branch as well as state and federal laws. Since 1803, the Supreme Court

judicial review
the right of the Supreme Court to find government actions or laws unconstitutional

has overturned more than one hundred federal laws and more than one thousand state laws.

The power of judicial review allows the Supreme Court to interpret the Constitution in new ways in order to meet the needs of a changing nation. It also allows the Supreme Court to reverse previous Supreme Court decisions. Decisions made by judicial review sometimes affect history. For example, two major cases, *Plessy v. Ferguson* and *Brown v. Topeka Board of Education,* affected the civil rights and freedom of millions of African Americans. Both cases were interpretations of the same clause in the Fourteenth Amendment. This clause says that states cannot deny people "the equal protection of the laws." How did judicial review of these two cases force many states to change their laws?

In the 1896 case called *Plessy v. Ferguson,* the Supreme Court used the Fourteenth Amendment to allow **segregation.** A segregation law in Louisiana separated African American people and white people in trains. In 1896, the Supreme Court ruled that this law was constitutional if the separate places for African Americans were of equal quality to the places for whites. After that, many states used the decision to pass

segregation
the separation of people based on race

Even water fountains were segregated before Plessy v. Ferguson.

African American students had to be escorted by police in order to enter school safely.

segregation laws. However, no one enforced the laws to make sure the places were equal. They often were not.

In 1954, in a case called *Brown v. Topeka Board of Education*, the Supreme Court reversed the 1896 decision. It used judicial review to overturn segregation laws. The 1954 decision said separate schools for African Americans and whites could never be equal, and the Fourteenth Amendment makes all segregation laws unconstitutional. Based on that decision, many **desegregation** laws were passed. States no longer have separate schools, trains, and restaurants for different people.

desegregation
ending the separation of people based on race

The Judicial Branch and Democracy

The Framers of the Constitution planned the judicial branch as part of the separation of powers. The judicial branch can prevent the abuse of power by Congress and the executive branch by declaring their laws and actions unconstitutional. The Constitution protects our freedom by giving every American the right to due process. Americans who do not receive due process in trials in lower courts can appeal to higher courts and even to the Supreme Court.

89

Comprehension — *Reviewing Important Facts*

Match the sentence in **Group A** with the word or phrase from **Group B** that the sentence explains. Write the letter of the correct answer on the blank.

Group A

_____ 1. This is one goal of the Constitution.

_____ 2. These trial courts are for federal crimes.

_____ 3. Decisions of this court cannot be appealed.

_____ 4. The Supreme Court decided that this idea in the First Amendment does not allow prayers in public school.

_____ 5. This person leads the Supreme Court.

_____ 6. This case allowed separate but equal public places for African Americans and whites.

_____ 7. This power allows the Supreme Court to overturn unconstitutional laws.

_____ 8. This case said separate schools for African Americans and whites are unconstitutional.

Group B

a. judicial review

b. *Plessy v. Ferguson*

c. District Courts

d. *Brown v. Topeka Board of Education*

e. separation of church and state

f. Chief Justice

g. "to establish justice"

h. Supreme Court

Critical Thinking — *Distinguishing Relevant Information*

Imagine that you must explain to a friend how the Supreme Court interprets and applies the Constitution. Read each sentence below and on the next page. Decide which sentences are relevant to what you will say. Put a check in front of the four relevant sentences.

_____ 1. The Supreme Court can decide which state laws must be changed.

_____ 2. Supreme Court decisions set precedents that are used to decide other cases.

_____ 3. The Supreme Court works from October through June.

_____ 4. Cases from Courts of Appeal can be brought to the Supreme Court.

_____ 5. Laws passed by Congress can be overturned by the Supreme Court.

_____ 6. Decisions made by the Supreme Court cannot be appealed.

_____ 7. Congress decides the salaries of Supreme Court justices.

_____ 8. The Supreme Court can overturn the actions of a President.

_____ 9. The words "equal justice under law" are on the Supreme Court building.

_____ 10. All justices must understand the Constitution.

Vocabulary — _Writing With Vocabulary Words_

Use seven or more words or phrases from the box to write a paragraph that tells how the federal court system promotes justice.

due process	**overturn**	**segregation**
precedents	**judges**	**judicial review**
appealed	**desegregation**	**justices**

_____

_____

_____

_____

_____

_____

_____

_____

Chapter 10

How a Bill Becomes a Law

Consider As You Read

- What steps are needed to pass a bill through both houses of Congress?
- What can the President do with a bill that has been passed by Congress?
- Why are compromises necessary in order to pass laws?

Congress passed a law in 1990 that affected television watching for children. The new law limited the number of commercials that could be shown during programs for children. This new law, like every law, first began as a bill that was introduced in one house of Congress. As a bill it went through many steps in order to become a United States law. Many bills, like the one to limit television commercials, are public bills that are written to help the nation. Other bills are private bills that are passed to help just one or a few people. Thousands of bills are introduced during each term of Congress, but most of them never become laws. Every bill must go through many steps before it can become a new law for the nation.

The President often signs bills into law during ceremonies at the White House.

Senators answer questions about bills that are being introduced in Congress.

Introducing a New Bill

Ideas for bills come from the President, department leaders, and the thousands of letters that citizens write to their senators and representatives. Only a senator or a representative can introduce a new bill to Congress. Every new bill starts with an introduction in either the Senate or the House of Representatives. We will follow a bill that starts in the House. A bill that starts in the Senate goes through the same process.

Every bill must have three readings in order to be passed by the House. During the first reading, the bill is introduced in the House. Although the introduction of a bill is called the first reading, the bill is not read aloud. Instead, it is given a number and a title and then sent to the correct committee for further study.

There are many different kinds of committees in both houses. Bills about veterans are considered by the Veteran Affairs Committee, and bills about taxes are sent to the House Ways and Means Committee.

Committees decide what happens to each bill. First, the committee studies the bill. Most bills are killed in committees and are never voted on by Congress. However, sometimes a committee decides the new bill should be studied further. The bill is then sent to a **subcommittee.** The House has about 140 subcommittees, and the Senate has about 100.

The members of the subcommittee study the bill to find out if the nation needs the bill and how it will help the nation. The subcommittee listens to opinions of people who will be affected by the bill. The subcommittee also hears opinions about the bill from people in their states and from leaders of government agencies. These opinions help the subcommittee decide what to do with the bill. Most of the time, the subcommittee decides to kill the bill. Sometimes a subcommittee recommends passage of the bill and sends that bill to the floor of the House for **debate**. The subcommittee sometimes **amends** the bill before sending it on to the House. Then it is up to the members of the House to pass the bill.

The Second Reading, Debating, and Voting

The bill receives a second reading on the floor of the House. This time the bill is read aloud to the members of the House. After the reading the debate on the bill begins. Changes are often made in a bill during the debate, and amendments are sometimes added to the bill.

Due to the large number of representatives in the House, there are strict rules to control debates. The amount of time a representative can speak is limited. The Speaker of the House controls the debates.

Debates are freer in the Senate since the membership is much smaller. Senators can remain on the Senate floor to speak for as long as they wish. As they debate, they share ideas that are often used to improve the bill. When the debates have ended, the senators are ready to vote.

Since there is no limit to how long a senator can talk, senators sometimes "talk a bill to death." **Filibusters** are used to stop the Senate from voting on a bill. During one filibuster a senator read from the phone book. The longest filibuster by one person was by Senator Strom Thurmond in 1957. Thurmond's filibuster lasted 24 hours, as he tried, without success, to stop the Senate from passing a civil rights law. One filibuster by several senators lasted about three weeks. Senate rules make it difficult to end a filibuster, so it often works to kill a bill.

During one filibuster in 1960 Senators slept on cots.

The Third Reading and Voting

After the debates end, the bill is printed and given a third reading. This time, only the title of the bill is read to the House. Bells ring in the House to call members who are in their office or in committee meetings to vote.

A majority vote is needed to pass a bill in either the House or the Senate. Members of Congress often vote for those bills that their political party wants to pass. All voters can learn the voting records of their senators and representatives. Members of Congress are often judged by the way they vote. **Constituents** want to know what bills their senators and representatives have voted for.

constituents
voters

The Final Steps for Passing a Bill

After a bill is passed by the House, it is sent to the Senate. The bill must follow the same steps if it begins in the Senate. So once again the bill is assigned to committees, debated on the floor of the Senate, voted on, and sent to the other house.

Both houses of Congress must pass the same version of a bill in order for it to become a law. Sometimes the bill will be

conference committee
committee with members
from both houses

changed in the second house of Congress. Since both houses must pass the same version of the bill, the bill will then be sent to a **conference committee.** Members of both houses make changes to the parts of the bill that were different. These compromises are written into the bill. Then both houses vote on the compromise bill. If the bill is passed by both houses, and most compromise bills are passed, it is then sent to the President of the United States.

As the nation's chief lawmaker, the President must read every bill that is passed by Congress. He has ten days, without counting Sundays, to make a decision about the bill. The President must do one of four things with the bill. First, he can sign the bill, and it will become a new law for the nation. Second, the President can keep the bill for ten days without signing it, and the bill will still become a law. Third, the President can use his veto power to prevent the bill from becoming a law, but he must explain why he vetoed the bill. Finally, the President has pocket veto power to stop a bill from becoming a law. This means that if Congress adjourns before

Committees meet to discuss bills and to study issues.

President Clinton signs a bill into law.

the ten days have passed and the President has done nothing with the bill, then the bill cannot become a law.

What happens to bills that are vetoed by the President? Congress can override the President's veto if two thirds of the members in both houses vote for the bill. It is very difficult to get enough votes from both houses to override a veto.

Many times Congress prepares a compromise version of the defeated bill. Congress uses the reasons behind the President's veto to prepare the compromise bill. The President often accepts the compromise bill, and the nation has a new law. But many times the President tells Congress he will veto a bill even before the bill goes to him. Then Congress can write a bill that the President will sign.

Lawmaking Is Democracy in Action

The goal of every Congress is to pass the best possible laws for the nation. It is not easy to pass a new law, and there are many times during the long process when bills can be killed. Because it is difficult for a bill to pass through so many steps, most laws that are passed are laws that many people want and support.

It is not enough for Congress to pass good laws for the nation; those laws must be enforced. The huge executive bureaucracy, with its many departments and agencies, carries out the laws of Congress.

American lawmaking is democracy in action. Members of Congress are the voice of the American people. Since lawmakers care about pleasing their constituents, they usually pass the kinds of laws the voters want. Debates and compromises in Congress allow all members to share ideas and work for the good of the nation. The system of checks and balances prevents Congress from passing laws that will limit the freedom of the people.

How a Bill Becomes a Law

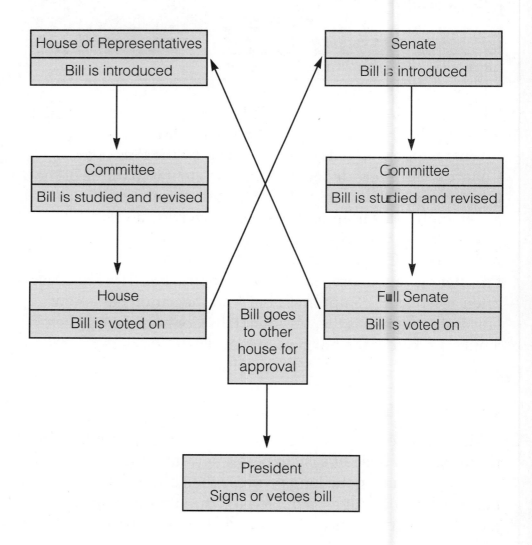

Comprehension — *Who Said It?*

Read each statement. Then look in the box for the person who might have said it. Write the name of the person you choose on the blank after each sentence.

constituent	committee member	President
U.S. Representative	U.S. Senator	

1. "I will introduce a tax bill in the House to pay for the new education programs."

   _____

2. "Since we don't want to kill this bill, let's send it to a subcommittee for further

   study." _____

3. "I don't want this bill to be passed, so I will try to kill it with a filibuster."

   _____

4. "I will write to my representative about why the nation needs a law to limit

   commercials during television shows for children." _____

5. "I vetoed the minimum wage bill because it would make salaries too high for many

   business owners." _____

Vocabulary — *Match Up*

Choose a word or phrase from the box to complete each sentence. Write that word or phrase on the blank.

filibuster	debate	conference committee
constituent	amend	subcommittee

1. A _____ is a person who is represented by a senator or representative.

2. A _____ is a committee that is part of a larger committee.

3. During a _____ , a senator speaks for a very long time from the Senate floor.

4. When members of Congress _____ , they state their reasons and arguments.

5. A subcommittee can change, or _____ , a bill.

6. Members from both houses meet in a _____ to write a compromise bill.

Critical Thinking — *Drawing Conclusions*

Read the paragraph below and the sentences that follow it. Put a check in front of the conclusions that can be drawn from the paragraph.

Every new bill begins with a first reading to introduce it to the House or Senate. Then it is sent to a committee. Most bills are killed in committees, but some are sent to subcommittees for further study. If the committee wants to pass the bill, it is sent to the House or Senate for debate, and then a vote is taken. When the bill is passed by one house, it must go through the same steps in the other house. After it passes through both houses, it must go to the President before it can become a law.

_____ 1. It takes many steps for a bill to become a law.

_____ 2. Compromises help a bill pass through both houses.

_____ 3. A conference committee includes members of both houses.

_____ 4. The President can sign or veto each bill.

_____ 5. Committees play an important part in passing bills.

_____ 6. Many people read and discuss a bill before it becomes a law.

_____ 7. Bills often die in committee.

Skill Builder

Reading a Bar Graph

A **bar graph** uses bars of different lengths and colors to show facts. The bar graph below compares the number of regular vetoes, the number of pocket vetoes, and the number of vetoes overridden during the terms of four Presidents. Look at the bar graph. Then write the answer to each question.

Vetoes and Overridden Vetoes of Four Presidents

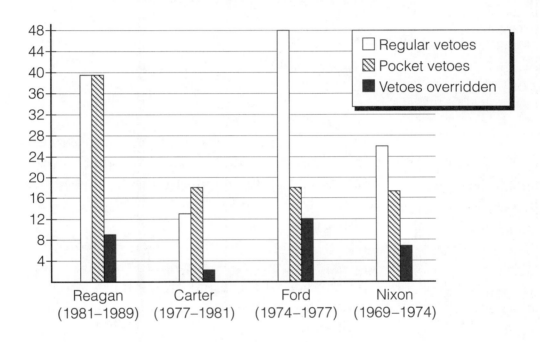

1. What Presidents are shown in this bar graph? _____

2. Of the four Presidents, who served the longest? _____

3. Who had the most total vetoes? _____

4. Who had the most vetoes overridden? _____

5. Who had the most pocket vetoes? _____

6. Who had the same number of regular and pocket vetoes? _____

7. Who had the fewest differences with Congress on what should be new laws?

   How do you know? _____

   _____

Linda Brown

Brown vs. Topeka Board of Education

In 1954, Linda Brown of Topeka, Kansas, wanted to go to the all-white school. Segregation laws forced her to go to an all-black school farther from home. Linda's parents took the Topeka Board of Education to court to fight for Linda's right to go to the all-white school. The case was appealed to the Supreme Court. Here is part of the 1954 Supreme Court decision in which the justices said that separate-but-equal laws were against the Fourteenth Amendment to the Constitution.

minors
people under sixteen years of age

obtaining
getting

admission
entrance

plaintiffs
people bringing the case to court

contend
argue

deprived of
not allowed

tangible factors
things seen by the eye; here, buildings, teachers, what is being taught

Minors of the Negro race, through their legal representatives, seek the aid of the courts in **obtaining admission** to the public schools of their community. . . . They had been denied admission to schools attended by white children under laws requiring or permitting segregation according to race. . . .

The **plaintiffs contend** that segregated public schools are not "equal" and cannot be made "equal," and that hence they are **deprived of** the equal protection of the laws. . . .

There are findings below that the Negro and white schools involved have been equalized, or are being equalized. . . . Our decision, therefore, cannot turn on merely a comparison of these **tangible factors** in the Negro and white schools involved in each of the cases. We must look instead to the effect of segregation itself on public education. . . .

It is doubtful that any child may . . . be expected to succeed in life if he is denied . . . an education. Such an opportunity, . . . is a right which must be made available to all on equal terms.

We come then to the question presented: Does segregation of children in public schools solely on the basis of race . . . deprive the children of the minority group of equal educational opportunities? We believe that it does. . . .

Such considerations apply . . . to children in grade and high schools. To separate them from others of similar age and

Today schools are integrated, in part because Linda Brown fought for an equal education.

qualifications solely because of their race **generates** a feeling of **inferiority** . . . that may affect their hearts and minds in a way unlikely ever to be undone. . . .

We conclude that . . . separate educational **facilities** are inherently unequal. . . . We have now announced that such segregation is a denial of the equal protection of the laws. . . .

generates
causes

inferiority
being less than equal

facilities
buildings, teachers, classrooms

The Supreme Court ruled that the Fourteenth Amendment protects the right of all people to an equal education. This Supreme Court decision forced states throughout the nation to integrate their public schools. Linda Brown was then able to go to the school of her choice.

Write About It

On a separate sheet of paper, write a paragraph that explains why you think this Supreme Court decision was important. Explain whether or not you think the changes it caused were for the best and why.

UNIT 3
State and Local Government

Every state in the United States has its own constitution. Like the Constitution of the United States, they were written to protect the rights and freedom of the people. All state constitutions have some things in common. They all divide the powers of government into three branches. The branches of state governments check and balance one another. The power of the government is limited. Every constitution also has a Bill of Rights. And, like the Constitution of the United States, all state constitutions give the power to the people.

Every town and city also has its own government. These local governments touch your life in more ways than the state and federal governments do. The local government plays a part when you are born, when you go to school—even when you wash the dishes! When you become involved in government, it will most likely be at the local level.

Have You Ever Wondered . . .

- The United States Constitution has lasted two hundred years, but many state constitutions have been rewritten. Why haven't state constitutions lasted longer?

- The United States Constitution does not list the powers of state governments. What powers do state governments have?

- All districts in a state are drawn to give people equal representation. Why is this important for democracy?

- Certain thirteen-year-olds can drive in Montana, but people in Massachusetts cannot drive until they are 16½. Why do states have laws that are different from those in other states?

- The United States Constitution did not create local governments. Why are there thousands of them?

This unit will answer all of these questions. You will compare state constitutions with the United States Constitution. You will learn how state governments serve the people. You will understand how the legislative, executive, and judicial branches of government work together in state government. You will read about different types of local governments that are found across the nation. As you read this unit, think about the ways that state and local governments protect American freedom as they provide services to their people.

Chapter 11

Federalism's Other Side

Consider As You Read

- How are state constitutions like the United States Constitution? How do they differ?
- What powers do state governments have? What powers do they lack?

People use the services of their state governments every time they go to a public school, travel on a state highway, or visit a state park. Most people have more direct contact with their state governments than with the federal government.

The Framers of the Constitution planned a federal government to rule the entire nation and separate state governments to govern each state. The fifty states that form the United States differ from each other in size, population, geography, and natural resources. Rhode Island and Alaska are two examples of how states can vary. Rhode Island earns money through **industry** and manufacturing. Although Alaska has only about half as many people as Rhode Island, it covers the largest area of any state. Alaska earns much of its money from mining oil, natural gas, and other minerals. The governments in Alaska and Rhode Island have passed

industry
businesses

Oil from Alaska is carried through pipes to other parts of the United States.

Here the Massachusetts legislature meets.

different laws that meet the needs of the people living there. Since all states differ from each other, they need their own governments to meet their special needs.

Fifty State Constitutions

Just as the United States has a constitution, each of the fifty states has its own constitution. All state laws must agree with the state's constitution. However, the United States Constitution is the highest law for the nation, and all state constitutions and laws must agree with the United States Constitution. The *Brown v. Topeka Board of Education* decision is a good example of how the United States Constitution is the nation's highest law. After the Supreme Court ruled that school segregation laws were unconstitutional, many states had to change their laws and **integrate** their public schools.

integrate
bring together people of all races

The fifty state constitutions are similar to the United States Constitution in six ways. First, each state constitution creates a limited government. Second, in every state there is a separation of power into three branches of government. Third, each state government has checks and balances. Fourth, each state constitution has a bill of rights. Fifth, amendments can be added to all state constitutions. Sixth, all state constitutions are built on the idea of popular sovereignty. In every state, the power of government comes from the people, and people use their power when they vote in elections.

Bicycle Safety

The fifty state constitutions also differ from the United States Constitution. The United States Constitution has fewer than 10,000 words, while most state constitutions are far longer. The Framers planned the nation's Constitution as a flexible set of guidelines that could be interpreted to meet the needs of a changing nation. State constitutions are less flexible because they are written with many rules and details that explain exactly how state governments should work. For example, some state constitutions include the salaries of important officials. But salaries that were decided long ago are no longer enough for today's government leaders. So many state constitutions have been changed several times.

Only nineteen states now use their original constitutions. All other states have rewritten their constitutions at least once. Louisiana has written eleven constitutions since it first became a state. Only 27 amendments have been added to the United States Constitution. Most states have added far more amendments to their constitutions.

Powers of the State Governments

The United States Constitution explains only those powers the state governments do not have. It does not list the powers that do belong to the states. Instead, the Tenth Amendment in the Bill of Rights says that the states and the people have all powers that are not given to the federal government. The powers of the states have grown and been accepted over time.

States have the power to establish local governments in cities and towns. They can create public school systems and state court systems. States can pass tax laws and collect taxes to pay for state programs.

States have the power to make laws needed to protect the health, safety, and well-being of their people. To promote safety, states pass traffic safety laws, bicycle safety laws, and enforce laws through the state police. To protect the health of the people, state laws require health inspections of restaurants. State hospitals provide health care. To protect the well-being of the population, states have laws against robbery and murder. Teachers, doctors, lawyers, plumbers, and other professionals must meet requirements to get state certificates or licenses. In this way, the state governments make sure that these professionals will work to help the people in the state.

The Connecticut House of Representatives meets.

The United States Constitution denies certain powers to the states. States cannot print their own money or manufacture coins. Remember that at one time many states had their own money, and it was very confusing when people traveled from one state to another. States cannot go to war against another nation, nor can they make foreign treaties. Only the federal government can go to war or make treaties with other nations. States cannot tax goods that are sent from one state to another. The Framers felt that the states should be able to work together and trade together without any problems.

State Governments Serve the People

Every state government has three branches: the legislative, executive, and judicial. To meet the needs of the state, the legislature makes laws, the executive branch enforces laws, and the judicial branch interprets the laws. Citizens can attend public hearings to learn how members of their legislature deal with state problems.

State agencies are part of a state's executive branch and carry out the laws made by state legislatures. Some state agencies control prisons, protect state parks, and enforce traffic and driving laws.

The education agency is the largest agency in every state. The largest amount of money in a state's budget is used for education. The education agency decides how many days students must attend school each year. It decides what subjects will be studied at each grade, gives money for programs for students with disabilities, and sets requirements for high school graduation. In some states, education agencies prepare tests for different grade levels and subjects. Some states require students to pass state exams in order to graduate from high school. Every state has at least one state university that is run by its education agency.

State governments try to solve difficult problems such as protecting the **environment.** All states must find ways to protect their air, land, and water from pollution. Although the federal government has passed laws to control pollution, the states are creating their own laws and programs to protect their environment. Many states are being stricter than the federal government about solving the pollution problem. Because smog and air pollution are serious problems in parts of California, that state now has strict air pollution laws. Oregon has passed laws to protect its rivers. States can help protect their environment by finding safe ways to dispose of garbage. A number of states have passed laws to dispose of some garbage through recycling. Two of those states, Florida and Pennsylvania, now require that all glass bottles, newspapers, and aluminum cans be recycled.

Many kinds of state laws have been passed because of the hard work of the people of each state. It is at the state and local levels of government that you can have the most impact on how your government is run.

environment
land, air, and water

Many states have very strict recycling laws.

110

Vocabulary — *Writing With Vocabulary Words*

Use six or more words in the box to write a paragraph that tells about five ways that state governments serve the people.

industry	integrate	education	environment
constitution	court systems	traffic	health care
licenses	professionals	pollution	recycling

_____

_____

_____

_____

_____

_____

_____

Comprehension — *Write the Answer*

Write one or more sentences to answer each question.

1. Why does each state need its own constitution? _____

_____

2. What are three ways that state constitutions are like the United States Constitution?

_____

_____

3. What are three powers of state governments? _____

_____

_____

4. What is one power that is denied to state governments? Why is it denied? _____

_____

_____

5. What are three responsibilities of state education agencies? _____

_____

_____

6. How have two states tried to protect their environment? _____

_____

Critical Thinking — *Cause and Effect*

Choose a cause or an effect from **Group B** to complete each sentence in **Group A.** Write the letter of the correct answer on the blank.

Group A

1. The United States Supreme Court ruled that segregation laws were

   unconstitutional, so _____ .

2. The United States Constitution is a

   flexible document, so _____ .

3. _____ , so many states have had to rewrite their constitutions.

4. California had serious problems with

   the environment, so _____ .

5. _____ , so many states have passed laws to stop pollution.

6. States must protect public safety, so

   _____ .

Group B

a. State constitutions have too many details to be flexible.

b. State police enforce traffic laws.

c. Many states integrated their schools.

d. The federal government is not very strict about protecting the environment.

e. It has served the nation for two hundred years.

f. It passed strict air pollution laws.

Skill Builder

Reading a Bar Graph

The bar graph below shows the number of workers in five different groups. It shows these workers for the four regions of the United States. Study the bar graph. Then answer the questions.

Number of State Workers in Five Groups, 1987

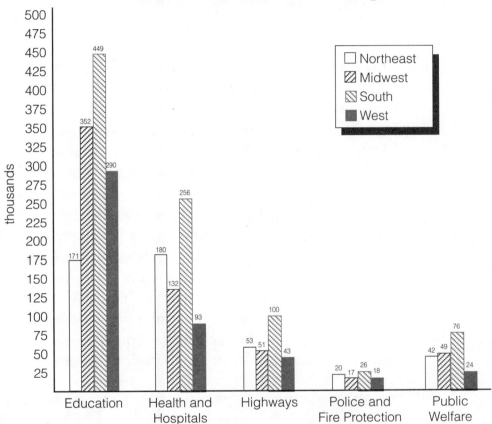

1. Which region has the most workers in education? Which has the fewest?

_____

2. How many employees in the Northeast work in Highways? _____

3. Which region has 26,000 workers in Police and Fire Protection? _____

4. Which region has the fewest workers overall? How do you know? _____

_____

5. Which region has the most workers overall? How do you know? _____

_____

Chapter 12

State Governments At Work

Consider As You Read

- How are state laws passed, and how can citizens take part in the lawmaking process?
- What is the job of the governor of each state?

Each state makes laws to meet its special needs. Montana is a large state with a small population and little public transportation. Young teenagers in rural areas had a hard time traveling to school. So Montana's legislature decided that thirteen-year-olds who live in areas far from school bus transportation could get a special driver's license that allows them to drive to a school bus stop. Because of that law, Montana now has the youngest drivers in the nation. Massachusetts is a small state with a large population. Since all areas of Massachusetts have school buses, teenagers have less need to drive cars than teenagers do in Montana. Because many cities have difficult traffic problems, Massachusetts lawmakers decided teenagers must be mature enough to drive. The laws in Massachusetts require teenagers to be 16½ years old when they apply for a junior driver's license.

Every state writes its own laws for when people can become drivers.

114

The legislature of Missouri meets in the capitol building in Jefferson City.

Massachusetts has the highest age requirement in the nation. The laws of Montana and Massachusetts are examples of how state governments try to meet the needs of their people.

The Legislative Branch of State Government

Every state but Nebraska has a two-house legislature where state laws are made. Nebraska has a one-house legislature. In every other state, the legislatures have an upper house, usually called the senate, and a lower house, usually called the house of representatives. State senates always have fewer members than the house of representatives. Every state is **apportioned** into large senate districts and smaller lower-house districts. District lines are drawn to give all people in a state equal representation.

apportioned
divided

State legislatures follow most of the same steps to pass state laws as Congress does. First a bill is proposed in one of the two houses of the state legislature. Then the bill is assigned to a committee for study. Committee members listen to citizens tell how they feel about the bill. A committee can kill a bill or it can approve the bill and send it back for debate and a vote. If the bill is passed in one house, it is then sent to the other house of the legislature.

Bills that are passed by both houses are then sent to the governor. The governor can either sign the bill so that it becomes a law or veto the bill to prevent it from becoming a law. North Carolina is the only state that does not allow the governor to veto a bill. Unlike the federal government, most states permit item vetoes by the governor. The item veto allows the governor to veto one part of the bill and allow other parts of the bill to become law. It is possible for the legislature to override the governor's veto. This does not happen often.

Citizens Get Involved

Citizens are much more involved in the lawmaking process at the state level than at the federal level. In many states, people can use the **initiative** method to propose laws. The initiative method allows a citizen or a group of citizens to use a petition to propose a law. If the required number of people in the state sign the petition, it is voted on in the next state election. The proposed law in the petition becomes a state law if it receives a majority of the votes in the election. Some states require initiatives to be passed by the legislature. If the legislature does not pass the initiative, then citizens can vote in a state election for it to become a law.

The **referendum** method also allows citizens to help in the lawmaking process. In many states, citizens vote in elections on certain kinds of laws that have been passed by the state legislature. Amendments and laws for borrowing money often require a referendum. The federal government, unlike the state governments, does not allow lawmaking through initiatives and referendums.

The Executive Branch of State Governments

Governors lead the executive branch in every state. The executive powers of the governors allow them to make state policies that are presented to the legislature in the "State of the State" speeches. Governors also prepare state budgets. They can call up the state's **militia,** or National Guard, to deal with emergencies like floods and riots. In many states, governors have the power to appoint many officials to the executive branch.

Governors also have legislative and judicial powers. They can propose bills and veto laws. In some states, the governors appoint many state judges. A governor can pardon people

initiative
proposed law

referendum
a proposed law that citizens must vote on

The state militia helps out in an emergency such as a flood.

militia
group of soldiers not belonging to the armed forces and used for special purposes

L. Douglas Wilder of Virginia became the first African American governor in the United States.

who have committed state crimes. A governor can reduce the **sentences** of people who are **convicted** of crimes.

Governors have other responsibilities. They serve as the state's leader for their political party. A governor is the state's chief of state. As chief of state, the governor attends many ceremonies, gives awards, and meets important leaders from the United States and other nations.

State constitutions list few requirements for people to become governors. They require governors to be United States citizens and qualified voters. Most governors are college graduates, and more than half are lawyers. Only thirteen governors have been women. In 1990, L. Douglas Wilder became the first African American governor when he won the election in Virginia. In the history of our nation, sixteen state governors have later become the President of the United States.

The Judicial Branch of State Governments

Every state has its own court system to interpret its laws and to hear court cases. Far more cases are heard in state courts than in federal courts.

There are three kinds of state courts. Trial courts are the lowest level of courts. Every state is divided into districts that are served by trial courts. There are many kinds of trial

sentences
punishments for crimes

convicted
found guilty

117

civil
having to do with things that are not considered illegal

criminal
having to do with things that are illegal

courts, and they hear **civil** as well as **criminal** cases. These courts hear cases that include divorce, problems with traffic, and arguments over money. There are also general trial courts in which jury trials are needed to decide murder and robbery cases.

The second group of courts are the intermediate courts of appeal. Most states have appeals courts. Cases that were decided in trial courts can be appealed to a court of appeals. The court of appeals decides whether the trial court followed due process. If appeals court judges decide that the accused was not treated fairly according to the law, they order a new trial for the accused.

The state supreme court is the third type of state court. The state supreme court is sometimes called by other names, but it is always the highest court in the state. A decision made by a state's supreme court is always final unless the case has to do with the United States Constitution. Those cases can be appealed to the United States Supreme Court for a final decision.

Unlike federal judges, who are appointed by the President of the United States, most state judges are chosen by voters in general elections. About one fourth of all state judges are appointed by governors. Some judges are appointed by state legislatures.

State Governments Serve the People

Thousands of state laws have been written to meet the special needs of each state. For example, in the 1960s, the people of Mississippi wanted more industries and factories in their state, so the legislature passed laws that helped the growth of industry. When New Jersey needed money for programs to help the elderly and the disabled, a law was passed in 1976 to allow casino gambling. Maryland's legislature has passed laws to clean up the polluted waters of Chesapeake Bay. Across the nation, state governments work hard to meet the needs of the people they serve.

The Supreme Court of Texas meets to discuss a case.

Using What You Learned

Vocabulary — *Match Up*

Choose a word or phrase from the box to complete each sentence. Write that word or phrase on the blank.

referendum	sentence	criminal	militia
item veto	due process	initiative	apportioned

1. Every state must be _____ into districts with equal populations.

2. A _____ allows citizens to vote on a bill in a state election.

3. A governor can use the power of the _____ to veto one part of a bill.

4. An _____ is a petition for a law by the citizens of a state.

5. The _____ is a group of soldiers that serve the state.

6. A _____ is a punishment for a crime.

7. A _____ case involves someone who is accused of committing a crime.

8. Cases that have not followed _____ go to an appeals court.

Comprehension — *Write the Questions*

Below are the answers for some questions from this chapter. Read each answer. Then write your own question above each answer. Use the question words to help you.

1. How _____ ?

   Every state except Nebraska has a two-house legislature.

2. How _____ ?

   The bill process follows the same steps as in the United States Congress.

3. What _____ ?

This lawmaking method involves getting a petition in order to propose a law.

4. When _____ ?

This lawmaking method is needed when states want to add an amendment or borrow money.

5. What _____ ?

They hear both civil and criminal cases.

Critical Thinking — *Categories*

Read the words in each group. Decide how they are alike. Write a title for each group on the blank beside each group. You may use the words in the box for all or part of each title.

Court System Powers	Governor Executive	Judicial Citizens

1. chief of state
   party leader of state
   leader of executive branch
   _____

2. trial courts
   intermediate courts of appeal
   state supreme court
   _____

3. initiative
   referendum
   attend public hearings
   _____

4. "State of the State" speech
   call up state militia
   prepare budget
   _____

5. appoints judges
   reduces sentences
   grants pardons
   _____

Chapter 13

Thousands of Local Governments

Consider As You Read

- How do local governments serve their people?
- What kinds of governments are found in cities and counties?

On October 17, 1989, a severe earthquake struck the city of San Francisco, California. For fifteen seconds the earth shook, and old buildings and highways collapsed. Immediately the city used its services to help people survive the damage from the earthquake. Police and fire fighters worked day and night to rescue people who were trapped under collapsed buildings and highways. Fortunately, San Francisco's government had passed laws that required buildings to be built in such a way that they would not collapse during an earthquake. Because of those laws, most buildings did not fall down.

San Francisco is just one of thousands of local governments. About 83,000 local governments across the United States provide many kinds of services to their people.

Safety laws kept more damage like this from happening during the San Francisco earthquake of 1989.

The Importance of Local Governments

Local governments are created by the states. The Framers of the Constitution planned federal and state governments, but they did not describe local governments. The states create local governments and give them the power to provide services to the people.

Local governments exist to solve local problems and provide services to communities. People use the services of local governments when they apply for marriage licenses, attend local public schools, borrow books from public libraries, and call for help from police and fire fighters. Most local governments provide communities with safe drinking water and electric and gas utility services. They fix damaged roads and provide help to needy people. Many local governments provide mass-transit services. In large cities, public transportation can include train, bus, and subway services. In smaller communities, bus service is often provided.

There are different types of local governments across the nation. These governments are found in the cities, towns, and **counties** of the nation.

counties
what states are divided into

The city government of Chicago provides this train.

A county board governs the county.

County Governments

Counties are created by state governments. They carry out state laws for local communities. All states except Connecticut and Rhode Island have county governments. At first county governments were planned to govern rural areas. Today many counties also include large cities. Los Angeles County in California, with about eight million people, is the largest county in the nation.

Most counties are governed by a board with five to nine members who are elected by the voters. Some boards have only three members, while some counties with large cities have more than one hundred board members. County governments include other elected officials, such as a **sheriff** and a **district attorney.** A county government does not have an elected executive leader.

County governments pass laws that meet local needs. Different counties in a state can have different laws. For example, New York's Nassau County has a traffic law that allows a driver to make a right turn while the traffic light is still red. In neighboring Queens County, where traffic is heavier, drivers must wait for the red light to turn green before making a right turn. County governments can pass tax laws to collect taxes. They provide police protection, public libraries, county parks, county hospitals, and other services for the people.

sheriff
the most important law officer of a county

district attorney
lawyer who works for the county

City Governments

American cities grow larger each year. Three fourths of the nation's people now live in urban areas. There are about 20,000 **municipal** governments for the nation's cities. City governments provide public services to large numbers of people.

A city is governed by a set of guidelines called a **city charter.** A city charter, like a constitution, can be changed by adding amendments. Some state governments write the charters for the cities, but most states allow cities to plan and write their own charters.

The most common plan for city government is the mayor-council plan. The mayor and the council members are elected by the city's voters. The mayor is the city's chief executive, and the council members form the city's legislature.

A mayor-council plan that gives the mayor many executive powers is called a strong mayor plan. The strong mayor plan is found in many large cities. Under this plan, the mayor can veto bills, appoint officials, make policies, and plan the budget.

Many small cities and towns with a mayor-council government give few powers to the mayor and many executive powers to the city council. This is called a weak mayor plan of government. Under a weak mayor plan, the city council makes laws, appoints officials, plans the budget, and creates policies. The mayor attends ceremonies and acts as another member of the council.

municipal
having to do with cities

city charter
plan for city government

Here the Chicago city council meets.

124

About 8,000 cities have a council-manager plan of government. This type of government is run very much like a business. Under this plan of government, there is a city council, a mayor with few executive powers, and a city manager. The city council members and the mayor are elected by voters. The city manager is chosen by the city council to carry out the policies made by the city council. The manager plans the city's budget, controls how money is spent, and hires and fires government officials. This type of government is usually found in smaller cities.

The Growth of Suburbs Changes the Cities

Since the 1940s, millions of Americans have moved from cities to nearby suburbs. After the war when more Americans began owning cars, it was easy to live in the suburbs and then travel to work in the cities. Many people moved to the suburbs to find a better way of life. Cheap houses were being built in the suburbs, and many people wanted to own their own homes.

In the 1940s people began moving out of cities into suburbs such as this one.

When middle class people left for the suburbs, people with fewer choices and lower incomes remained. Many businesses have left the cities in order to build new factories in the suburbs. Each year, cities are forced to spend more of their budget money on services for the needy.

Local Governments and the People

Local governments are the governments closest to the people. It is easier for citizens to work with their local governments than with their state or federal government. Citizens can sign petitions to change local laws and discuss government problems with city council members. They can attend city council meetings and write to their mayor about local problems. By voting in elections, citizens can help choose the best leaders for their government. Active citizens help their local governments provide better services for their people.

Comprehension — *Finish the Paragraph*

Use the words in the box to finish the paragraph. Write the words you choose on the blanks.

utilities	council-manager	officials
district attorney	public transportation	manager
sheriff	local	county

_____ governments are created by states to provide services to the people. These services can include libraries, _____ , and

_____ . All but two states have _____

governments. A county government includes elected _____ such as

a _____ and a _____ . About 8,000 American

cities now have a _____ government. The voters elect a mayor but

not the city's _____ , who has many executive powers.

Vocabulary — *Writing With Vocabulary Words*

Use seven or more words in the box to write a paragraph that tells how local governments work for their people.

suburbs	district attorney	utility	sheriff
counties	protection	city charter	electricity
transportation	libraries	fire fighters	traffic

_____

_____

_____

_____

Critical Thinking — *Fact or Opinion*

Read each sentence below. If the sentence is a fact, write **F** on the blank. If the sentence is an opinion, write **O** on the blank. If the sentence gives both a fact and an opinion, write **FO** on the blank and circle the part of the sentence that is an opinion.

_____ 1. An earthquake struck San Francisco in 1989, and the city's government handled the emergency very well.

_____ 2. There are differences in some traffic laws in Nassau and Queens counties, but Queens' law promotes safer driving.

_____ 3. County governments need mayors to serve as the executives.

_____ 4. There are thousands of local governments in the United States.

_____ 5. All but two states have county governments, which is the correct way for states to be governed.

_____ 6. The sheriff is the most important official in county government.

_____ 7. The council-manager plan of government has a council, a mayor, and a manager.

_____ 8. It is better for a mayor-council city government to have a strong mayor rather than a weak mayor.

_____ 9. Voters elect the mayor and the council members in a mayor-council government.

_____ 10. Millions of Americans have moved from cities to suburbs.

Skill Builder

Reading a Circle Graph

A **circle graph** shows how all of something is divided into parts. Most often a circle graph shows **percent,** or parts per one hundred. The circle graph on the left below shows what groups all city workers in the United States fall into. The circle graph on the right shows what percent of the total employee payments goes to each group.

Study both circle graphs. Then answer the questions below.

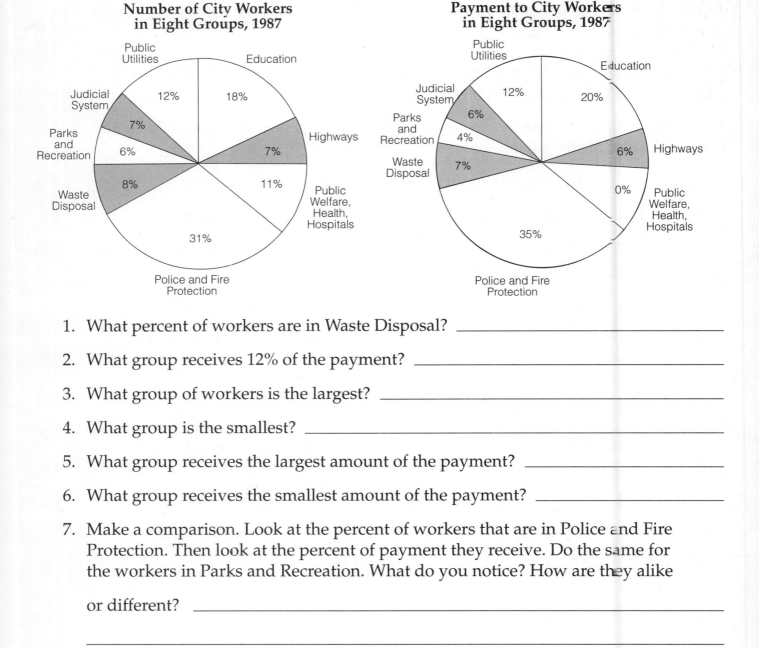

Number of City Workers in Eight Groups, 1987

Public Utilities 12%
Education 18%
Judicial System 7%
Parks and Recreation 6%
Highways 7%
Waste Disposal 8%
Public Welfare, Health, Hospitals 11%
Police and Fire Protection 31%

Payment to City Workers in Eight Groups, 1987

Public Utilities 12%
Education 20%
Judicial System 6%
Parks and Recreation 4%
Highways 6%
Waste Disposal 7%
Public Welfare, Health, Hospitals 0%
Police and Fire Protection 35%

1. What percent of workers are in Waste Disposal? _____

2. What group receives 12% of the payment? _____

3. What group of workers is the largest? _____

4. What group is the smallest? _____

5. What group receives the largest amount of the payment? _____

6. What group receives the smallest amount of the payment? _____

7. Make a comparison. Look at the percent of workers that are in Police and Fire Protection. Then look at the percent of payment they receive. Do the same for the workers in Parks and Recreation. What do you notice? How are they alike

    or different? _____

_____

Harold Washington

Chicago, Illinois

Harold Washington (1922–1987)

Many people in Chicago and around the nation did not think an African American could become mayor of the second largest city in the nation. But in 1983, Harold Washington was elected mayor of Chicago, Illinois.

When he was a boy, Harold Washington did small chores for the Democratic party. In college he became president of his class even though only five percent of the students in his class were African Americans. He served in the Illinois legislature and as a United States Representative.

In 1982, Washington entered the race for mayor of Chicago. Democrats had been mayor in Chicago since 1927. So Washington knew that if he could become the Democratic candidate, then he would have a good chance of becoming mayor. But he had to beat two white Democratic candidates. One was the woman who was then mayor. The other was the son of the man who had been mayor in Chicago for many years.

Forty percent of Chicago voters were African Americans. Washington knew that if he could get them to vote, he might become the Democratic candidate. He convinced many African Americans to vote. He became the Democratic candidate. He then went on to win the election for mayor.

Washington made some important changes in the city. First, he worked hard to involve many people in the government. He appointed more women, African Americans, and Hispanics than ever before. Second, mayors before Washington had appointed people because they were friends or because the mayor owed them something. Washington ended this practice. Finally, Washington was very careful about how money was spent. The city was able to save money during his term.

Washington was reelected as mayor in 1986. Less than a year later, he died of a heart attack. Washington encouraged thousands of African Americans in Chicago to vote. And since then, voters around the nation have elected many other African Americans.

This man is using a leafblower.

City Council Agenda
City of Sacramento, California
February 26, 1991

Sacramento is the capital of California. It is a city of about a half-million people. It is located on the Sacramento River, in the north central part of California. Sacramento has an eight-member city council and a mayor.

This meeting was held during the Persian Gulf War. Two issues on the agenda are related to that war. The members also discussed issues as varied as flood control, after-school programs for students, and banning leaf blowers.

Call to Order
Roll Call
Pledge of Allegiance

Notice: This city council meeting is being shown live this evening on the cable television government channel.

peripheral
outside edge

- Study of flood control improvements in south Sacramento
- Status report on the City's **Peripheral** Parking Pilot Program
- Approval of plans for Flood Control and Sewer Office Building
- Award of Bid No. 1499, Various Quantities and Types of Groceries for the 4th R **Latchkey Program** and Camp Sacramento

Latchkey Program
program for children who are home alone after school

- Approval of the Design Report for Sacramento Community/Convention Center Addition
- Setting of March 19, 1991, 7:30 p.m., for a hearing to determine the costs of destroying dangerous buildings
- Adopt emergency rules that would limit building heights within two blocks of Capitol Park
- Camp Sacramento—Fee increase of five percent user fee for mini-vacations, weekly session, and daily rates
- Ban the Blowers (leaf)

Sacramento is the capital of California, and this is its capitol.

- **Resolution condemning** discrimination against Arab Americans and people of the Muslim faith
- Resolution in support of our troops in the Persian Gulf
- Report from the Water Division of Public Works about Water Conservation 1991.

resolution
statement of agreement

condemning
disapproving of

Anyone in Sacramento may attend a city council meeting. Some people attend so that they can share their thoughts and ideas about issues on the agenda. However, they are allowed to talk for no more than three minutes.

Write About It

Choose one of the issues the city council discussed. On a separate sheet of paper, explain why you think a city government would be concerned about that issue. Describe what you think might be two or three arguments for or against that issue.

131

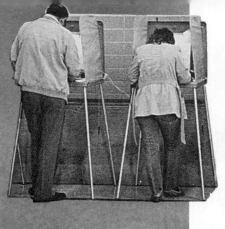

UNIT 4
Democracy at Work

The Framers wrote the Constitution to create a government "by the people and for the people." A government by the people depends on citizens using their voice to choose their leaders.

One way of making their voice heard is through elections. In 1787, only white men voted. Over the years amendments have been added to the Constitution to allow for all citizens, men and women of all races, to vote. The 26th amendment, added in 1971, says that the voting age is eighteen or older. Voting is an important part of democracy. By voting, all citizens have an equal voice in their government.

Citizens also make their voices heard through political parties. Two major political parties, the Democrats and the Republicans, choose people to run for office. Once elected, these people work to satisfy the constituents within their party.

Americans also affect government by writing letters and calling their representatives. Groups of people form to work for the special interests of voters. These groups try to influence lawmakers as they consider new bills.

In order for the government to be "by the people," the people must become involved. There are many ways for citizens to be a part of the government.

Have You Ever Wondered . . .

- The Framers opposed all political parties. Why are they a powerful force in our government?

- If the right to vote is so important, why do millions of people choose not to vote?

- Election campaigns last many, many months and cost millions of dollars. How do people pay for their campaigns?

- One woman started a group to fight drunk driving. How can one citizen have an effect on government?

The answers to these questions are in this unit. As you read the unit, you will learn about the many steps it takes to become a candidate in a presidential election. You will read about the difficult work that is part of an election campaign. You will understand the importance of television and newspapers in campaigns. You will read about groups that form to represent citizens by influencing lawmakers. As you read, think about the role of individuals in campaigns and elections.

Chapter 14

Political Parties and Voters

Consider As You Read
- What is the two-party system, and what role do third parties play?
- Who votes, and why do some people not vote?

Every four years, on the first Tuesday in November, voters decide who will lead the nation. Then, and at other times during the year, people take an active role in government by making their choice for federal, state, and local leaders. Months of campaigning and debating end on Election Day, and **candidates** wait for the voters to decide who will win or lose the elections. After the **polling places** close, people watch television to learn the election results. Only then do people know who will lead the nation.

The Two-Party System

Two political parties, the Republicans and Democrats, are an important part of every election. Political parties do five jobs for the nation. First, political parties set goals for the nation by developing a party **platform.** Second, in

candidates
people running for office

polling places
places to vote

platform
a political party's plan of action for the government

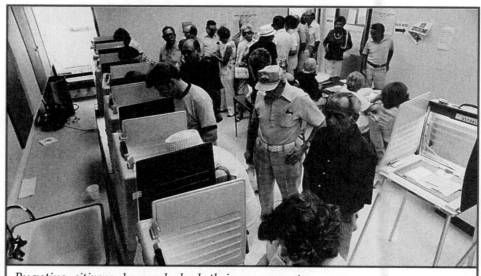

By voting, citizens choose who leads their government.

Through advertising, political parties inform the public.

order to carry out the platform, political parties are involved in elections. You will read about the election process in Chapter 15.

Third, parties inform the American people about the candidates and about the platform. They tell voters about problems they think the government needs to solve, and they make suggestions for solving those problems. Through advertising, speeches, and letters, parties are able to make their ideas known. Fourth, by getting their members into Congress and state legislatures, political parties put their platform ideas into action. Finally, parties are in competition with one another to get their members in government. Each party checks on the other to make sure that the party follows through on promises it made during campaigns.

The United States has a two-party system of government. The Democrats and Republicans have been elected to most positions in the government. The two-party system began more than two hundred years ago. The Framers of the Constitution and George Washington did not want to have any political parties because they felt parties would lead to fighting within the government. However, our two-party system began soon after the Constitution was written. One party, the Federalists, worked for the ratification of the Constitution. The opposing party, the Anti-Federalists, felt the Constitution gave too much power to the federal government. As time passed these parties changed. The

Federalist Party later became the Republican Party. The Anti-Federalists became the Democratic Party. The Republican and Democratic parties have changed their goals and platforms many times since they first began.

Third Parties

Republicans and Democrats control most elected government offices, but they are not the only political parties. The nation has smaller political parties called third parties. Third parties are started for three reasons. Some people start a third party because they have a different idea of how government should be organized than the Democrats and Republicans do. For example, the Libertarian Party was formed in 1971 to represent people who believe Americans should be free from the control of government. Second, third parties form to support one important issue such as environmental problems or women's rights. Third, sometimes members of the two major parties become unhappy with the way their party is doing things. So they decide to break away and start their own third party. This happened in 1968 when George Wallace left the Democratic Party, started the American Independent Party, and became its presidential candidate.

Theodore Roosevelt campaigned as a third-party candidate in the election of 1912.

Volunteers work for their political parties by doing many things.

Third parties can influence the government even though they have far less power than the two major parties. A third-party candidate has never been elected President of the United States, and few have been elected to Congress. Some third-party candidates have been elected to state and local governments. Third parties sometimes affect elections. If a third-party candidate gets enough votes to keep any candidate from winning a majority of votes, then another election between the top vote-getters may be held. Then those candidates still in the race work for votes that had gone to the third-party candidate.

Joining a Political Party

Every citizen can join a party because there are no dues and no age requirements for membership. The only requirement parties have is that people think of themselves as party members. Party members often do volunteer work for their party. Volunteers work at mailing political letters, making campaign phone calls, and raising campaign money. Political parties depend on volunteers to do much of the work during a campaign. In this way political parties are able to save money.

Who Can Vote?

Free and fair elections are important in every democracy. Since 1787, more groups of people have been given the right to vote. Amendments have been added to the Constitution allowing African Americans, women, and people who are eighteen years old to vote.

People must meet four requirements in order to vote in local, state, and national elections. The first requirement is that the voter must be at least eighteen years old. American citizenship is the second requirement in all states. Voters can be citizens by birth or through naturalization. Third, a person must live in the state for a certain amount of time, usually about thirty days. The fourth requirement is **registration.** All states except North Dakota require voters to register. When people register, their names are added to the list of voters for their state. This list is used to check off the names of people as they vote on Election Day. It is used to stop people from voting more than once, and it prevents people from voting if they do not meet requirements. Voters receive a voter registration card, which shows that they are able to vote.

registration
filling out a form

Nonvoting

In every election there are qualified voters who choose not to vote. In the 1992 presidential election, almost half of the nation's qualified voters did not vote. Many people feel that having so many voters who do not vote is a big problem since elections should speak for all Americans.

There are seven reasons why many people do not vote. First, people may feel they have not learned enough about the candidates and the issues in order to make choices at the polls.

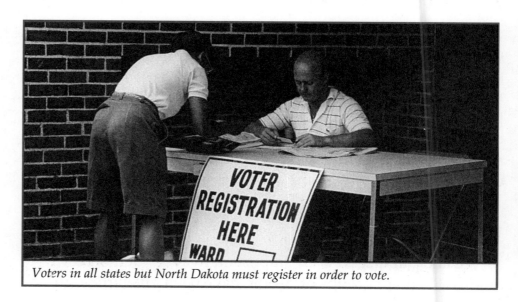

Voters in all states but North Dakota must register in order to vote.

They don't understand the differences between the candidates.

Second, some people feel that their one vote does not make a difference, so they don't bother to go to the polls. Third, some people either dislike all of the candidates, or they feel that both candidates are good choices, so they choose not to vote for either. Fourth, some people don't vote because they don't care very much about who wins or loses. They don't believe the election results will change the way government works. Fifth, people don't vote because they don't feel strong ties to a political party. They don't feel they should support a political party's candidate.

Sixth, there are people who want to vote but cannot do so. It is difficult for people with disabilities, seriously ill people, and people without transportation to get to the polls. Sometimes party volunteers drive these people to the polls. Finally, some citizens are not familiar with their state's registration process. They do not know how to become registered voters, and they do not bother to find out.

Voters

Who Are the Voters?

We do know what kind of person does vote in elections. The average voter is usually more than 35 years old, white, married, and has more education and income than most nonvoters. Voters are often party members who feel a strong tie to their party. They want to support their party's candidates and issues. The average voter believes each vote is important in deciding the nation's future.

There are many ways for voters to become informed about the candidates and their platforms. Newspapers, magazines, and television news are three common ways for voters to get information. Often candidates participate in debates. Watching these debates is an excellent way to learn about the candidates.

Democracy, as we have seen, depends on people being active in their government. Every year, in every part of the nation, citizens have the chance to vote for candidates and issues. Elections allow the United States to be a government by the people because voters make decisions for the nation. The voice of the American people is heard when they cast their votes on Election Day.

Comprehension — *Who Said It?*

Read each statement. Then look in the box for the person who might have said it. Write the name of the person you choose on the blank after each sentence.

party volunteer	average voter	nonvoter
candidate	third-party leader	

1. "My political party nominated me to run for governor in the state election."

   _____

2. "I don't understand the differences between the candidates in the election, so I will

   not vote in this election." _____

3. "I am more than 35 years old, I went to college, and I really want the candidate from
   my political party to win, so I must go to the polls and vote."

   _____

4. "I was not happy with the Democrats or Republicans, so I broke away and started

   my own political party." _____

5. "I work hard for my political party without being paid because I believe my party

   has the best goals for the United States." _____

Vocabulary — *Choosing Vocabulary*

Choose a word or phrase from the box to complete each sentence. Write that word or phrase on the blank.

platform	average	candidate	polling place
registration	third party	transportation	

1. A _____ is a person who runs for office in an election.

2. A party _____ contains the political party's main ideas and goals.

3. The place where people vote is called the _____ .

4. In all but one state, _____ is required before a person can vote.

5. Sometimes people leave one of the two major parties and form a

_____ .

6. Sometimes people do not vote because they have no _____ .

7. The _____ voter is over 35, married, and educated.

Critical Thinking — *Drawing Conclusions*

Read the paragraph below and the sentences that follow it. Put a check in front of the conclusions that can be drawn from the paragraph.

Political parties choose candidates and campaign for them to win elections. In Congress members of the same political parties sit together and work together. The President of the United States is the leader of his political party. Once in office a President appoints members of his party to be leaders in the executive branch.

_____ 1. Political parties are important in American government.

_____ 2. Congress is organized by political parties.

_____ 3. People who belong to the President's political party have a better chance of being appointed to the executive branch.

_____ 4. Third parties can affect election results.

_____ 5. Political parties are necessary for nominating and campaigning for candidates.

_____ 6. American government is controlled by a two-party system.

_____ 7. Political parties are involved in many ways in government.

Skill Builder

Comparing Circle Graphs

The two circle graphs below are about the voting population in the 1992 presidential election. Study and compare the two circle graphs. Then use the information in the graphs to answer the questions.

1992 Presidential Elections

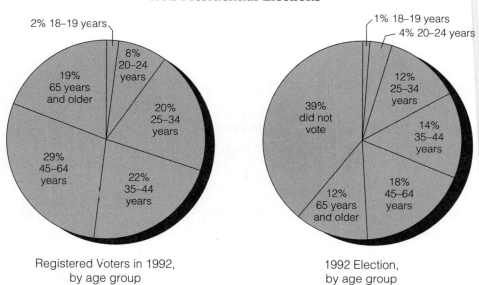

Registered Voters in 1992,
by age group

1992 Election,
by age group

1. What age group was the smallest group of people that actually voted?

_____

2. What age group were the two largest groups of people who actually voted?

_____

3. What percent of the people actually voted in 1992? _____

4. Of the registered voters in the 1992 election, what percent were 20–24 years old and actually voted?

_____

5. Compare the percentages of people in the 20–24 age group of registered voters with those who actually voted. Draw one conclusion from your comparison.

_____

_____

Chapter 15

Campaigns and Elections

Consider As You Read
- What is the campaign process?
- Why are campaigns expensive, and how do candidates pay for them?
- How do candidates influence voters?

News reporters were ready and waiting when George Bush made his announcement. He told reporters that he planned to become a Republican candidate in the 1988 presidential election. Within a few hours, news reports about Bush's decision had reached every part of the nation.

All candidates' campaigns begin when they announce their candidacy. It is just the beginning of a long process that has many steps. In this chapter we will look at that process.

Lyndon B. Johnson announced his candidacy for President in 1960. He became the Vice President with John F. Kennedy.

Nominating Presidential Candidates

As much as two years before the election, people announce their plans to become presidential candidates. Many people in each party will declare candidacy in both parties. But only one from each party can be on the **ballot** on election day. Once the announcements have been made, the difficult job of campaigning begins.

A political party can **nominate** only one person to be its presidential candidate for the general election. Since many people announce that they want to be their party's candidate, primary elections and a national party convention are held to select one candidate to represent each party. Delegates to the national convention elect one candidate who will be that party's choice for President.

At the **primary elections,** voters choose delegates to the convention, and in some states they vote on the candidate of their choice. All announced candidates can be on the ballot in the party's primary elections. In states that do not have primaries, people at political party meetings choose their delegates. Each announced candidate tries to win as many primary elections and as many convention delegates as possible.

As the months pass, candidates who lose important primary elections drop out of the presidential race. They realize they will not have enough delegate votes to win their party's nomination. Candidates who run out of campaign money also

ballot
a form used for voting

nominate
select; choose

primary elections
elections at state level that are held before the national election

Candidates, like Jesse Jackson, make thousands of speeches.

144

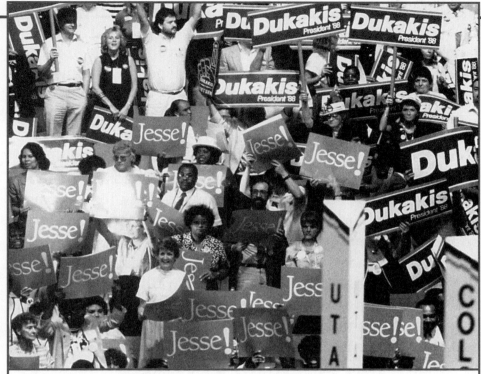

Delegates to the national convention vote for the candidate of their choice.

drop out of the race. By the time the national convention is held, only a few candidates from each party are left in the presidential race.

The Democrats and Republicans hold separate national conventions during the summer before the presidential election. The purpose of these conventions is to nominate one person to be the party's candidate in the presidential election and to decide on the party platform.

During the convention delegates from every state elect a candidate to represent the party in the November election. The person who wins the most delegate votes wins the party's nomination to be its presidential candidate. After winning the nomination, the presidential candidate chooses a party member to be the vice presidential candidate. Each candidate gives a speech during the convention, which is heard over television and radio by interested Americans.

Paying for Campaigns

After the conventions the presidential candidates continue their campaigns across the nation. These campaigns cost millions of dollars. The candidates know that to be elected they must become known to the millions of voters across the nation. They cannot reach all those people unless they have large amounts of money to pay for their campaigns. In 1988, George Bush and Michael Dukakis each spent a little more than 46 million dollars on their campaigns.

Campaign money is spent in five different ways. First, candidates spend millions of dollars on advertising. Advertising is probably the easiest way to reach the voters. But each television commercial or newspaper advertisement costs thousands of dollars. Each party also pays for campaign buttons, hats, bumper stickers, and posters for people who support that candidate.

rallies
large groups of people gathered for a political reason

Second, candidates travel to different states and speak with thousands of citizens at meetings and at **rallies.** Plane travel and hotel rooms are a big expense. Third, political parties rent many campaign offices in every state. Rent, telephone bills, and electric bills must be paid for every office. Fourth, professional campaign workers are paid large salaries to direct and manage the campaign. Although volunteers do lots of campaign work, professional managers, press secretaries, and speech writers are needed.

Fifth, campaigns are expensive because they last a long time. A campaign can begin two years before a general election when candidacy is first announced. For the next two years, money must be spent on all kinds of advertisements, travel expenses, campaign managers, and speech writers.

Paul Simon, a candidate for President in 1988, raised money at large dinners.

This was the first billboard put up for Richard Nixon, in 1959. It was put up in the town where he was born.

Sources of Campaign Money

Political parties work hard to raise millions of dollars for campaigns from citizens and from businesses. People pay to attend fund-raising events such as dinners and picnics. Candidates send letters and make phone calls asking for citizens to contribute large or small amounts of money to the campaign. Political action committees (PACs), which will be discussed in Chapter 16, also give large amounts of money to campaigns. The candidates themselves often spend their own money on their campaigns.

Congress has tried to limit campaign spending. It has passed laws to limit the amount of money individuals and PACs can contribute to presidential campaigns. These laws were passed because many people believed that the President might give special favors, such as jobs, to people who gave large amounts of money to the campaigns.

Since 1971, Congress has passed several laws to give **public funds** to presidential candidates. Public funds come from the nation's taxpayers. Public funds make it easier for candidates to pay for their campaigns. Because public funds can be given to candidates who are running in primary elections, it has become easier for people to become candidates in the primaries.

public funds
money from citizens

147

Influencing Public Opinion

As soon as candidates are nominated at the political party conventions, they begin working to influence voters and win their votes. Every day counts in the effort to win as many votes as possible. To win votes candidates must influence **public opinion.** By using advertisements and by traveling to meet voters, candidates hope to influence public opinion.

Propaganda is one of the methods used to influence public opinion. Propaganda uses facts, pictures, and sounds to persuade people how to vote. During a campaign, propaganda is used to create images about candidates and their opponents.

The **media** plays an important role in influencing public opinion. Candidates want to be seen and heard often on television and radio. Each party hires press secretaries to keep the media informed of its candidate's activities. Several television debates are held to help voters learn what each candidate thinks about important issues.

A presidential candidate needs the right image to be popular with the voters. Some members of the campaign staff are hired to help candidates improve their image. These staff members make sure the candidate wears the right clothes, has the right hairstyle, speaks well, and acts friendly.

Measuring Public Opinion

Candidates want to know if their advertising and campaign methods are working to win votes. They depend on public opinion polls to find out how well they are influencing voters. To take a public opinion poll, a small part of the population that is representative of the whole population answers questions. The answers given by the sample population show how most of the population would probably vote.

The results of public opinion polls are reported in the news. The polls show campaign managers how well their candidate is doing. If the poll shows that the opponent is winning, then the managers will plan different campaign methods to win more votes. The results of public opinion polls also influence the voters. When a poll tells voters which candidate is losing, many voters decide they would rather vote for the winning candidate.

public opinion
what the citizens think

propaganda
ways of persuading people

media
television, radio, newspapers, magazines

Candidate Nixon

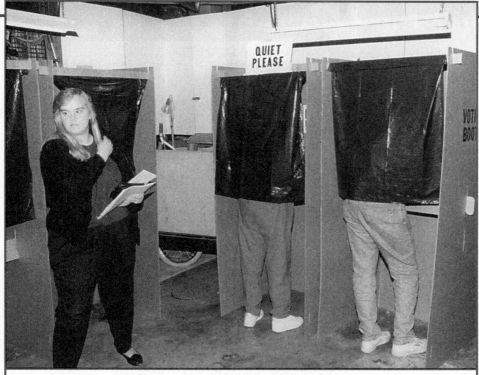

On Election Day, people vote for the candidate of their choice.

At the Voting Polls

After months of campaigning, Election Day finally arrives, and the voters cast their votes to choose the nation's next President. Registration is checked at the polling places before voters are allowed to vote. Campaigning is not allowed at the polling places.

Across the nation citizens cast their votes on secret ballots. Each person's freedom of choice at the polls is protected with secret ballots.

After all the voting polls in the nation have closed at night, the votes are counted and the winner is announced. Americans eagerly watch television and listen to radio to learn who their new President will be.

This long process of electing the nation's new President involves many people. But in the end, it is in the voting booth that all Americans have the opportunity to let their voice be heard.

Vocabulary — *Writing With Vocabulary Words*

Use six or more words in the box to write a paragraph that tells how candidates campaign to win elections.

ballot	public funds	nomination
political convention	public opinion	media
public opinion poll	propaganda	candidate
fund-raising		

_____

_____

_____

_____

_____

_____

_____

_____

Comprehension — *Write the Questions*

Below are the answers for some questions from this chapter. Read each answer. Then write your own question above each answer. Use the question words to help you.

1. What _____ ?

   Separate elections are held by the political parties in many states to choose delegates to the national convention.

2. What _____ ?

   During the summer before each presidential election, political party delegates meet to nominate a presidential candidate and write a party platform.

3. Why _____ ?

A presidential campaign must pay for television commercials, plane travel, campaign offices, and a campaign staff.

4. What _____ ?

Facts, pictures, and sounds are used to influence public opinion.

5. What _____ ?

In order to influence public opinion, campaigns create images about candidates and their opponents.

6. Why _____ ?

Campaign managers need to measure public opinion in order to know whether their campaign methods are winning votes.

7. What _____ ?

People go to polling places and vote on the candidates of their choice.

Critical Thinking — *Distinguishing Relevant Information*

Imagine you want to explain to a new American citizen how political campaigns try to influence public opinion. Read each sentence below. Decide which sentences are relevant to what you will say. Put a check in front of the four relevant sentences.

_____ 1. Every presidential candidate must choose a vice presidential candidate.

_____ 2. Candidates travel across the nation to meet thousands of voters.

_____ 3. Candidates use propaganda to persuade citizens not to vote for their opponents.

_____ 4. Public funds make it easier for candidates to enter primary elections.

_____ 5. Many people contribute to a candidate's campaign fund.

_____ 6. To win the party's nomination, a candidate must win many primaries.

_____ 7. Television commericals and newspaper advertisements are an important part of a campaign.

_____ 8. Campaign managers try to create the right image for their candidate.

Peggy Noonan (1950–   )

Peggy Noonan

On the campaign trail, candidates may give several speeches in one day. They do not have the time to write their own speeches. Sometimes they do not have the ability to write a good speech. They often hire people to write their speeches. One of these speech writers was Peggy Noonan.

Noonan began her career as a writer of television news programs. As a member of the Republican Party, Noonan admired Ronald Reagan and wanted to help him. So she was pleased when asked to join the White House staff as a speech writer. Noonan spent time listening to Reagan talk so that the speeches she wrote would sound like him. However, she did not write the President's speeches alone. Reagan and his staff provided the facts, and other speech writers helped. Then White House staff members corrected her work.

When George Bush announced his presidential candidacy, he asked Noonan to be one of his speech writers. Noonan wanted Bush to win, so she wrote campaign speeches for the primary elections. Bush asked her to write his acceptance speech for his nomination at the Republican National Convention. She spent weeks using Bush's ideas to write a moving speech. One of the phrases Noonan put in the speech, "a thousand points of light," became a phrase that Bush used often in his campaign. Noonan wrote many speeches for Bush throughout his campaign. In this way she helped Bush win the election.

George Bush gave his acceptance speech in August 1988.

Chapter 16

PACs and Interest Groups

Consider As You Read

- What are interest groups, and what role do they play in government?
- How do lobbyists influence lawmakers?
- In what ways do interest groups both help and harm the nation?

Candy Lightner decided to do all she could to keep drunk drivers off the roads after her daughter was killed by a drunk driver. Through the group she started, called Mothers Against Drunk Drivers, or M.A.D.D., Lightner worked for stricter laws to prevent drunk driving in her state of California. Since people across the nation contributed money to M.A.D.D., the organization had the money it needed to pay for television commercials and education programs to stop drunk driving. M.A.D.D. also influenced Congress to pass stricter laws to stop people from driving while drunk. Through M.A.D.D., Candy Lightner found a way to make her voice heard in American government.

Candy Lightner started M.A.D.D., an interest group to stop drunk driving.

The Purpose of Interest Groups

M.A.D.D. is just one of the many interest groups in the nation. Interest groups are organizations that people form in order to get laws passed that benefit the interests of the people they represent. For example, the Friends of the Earth interest group works for people who want to protect plants and animals. It pressures lawmakers to pass laws that keep land safe for wildlife. Interest groups usually work for only those issues that are of interest to their own members.

Different Types of Interest Groups

The nation's many interest groups can be divided into three types of groups. The first and largest group is based on business activity. Business groups include labor unions, farm groups, and professional organizations. These interest groups work to make sure their business can grow and continue to make money. These interest groups often provide other kinds of services to their members. These services can include medical care and programs to improve professional knowledge and job skills. For example, an interest group called the American Medical Association pressures the government to pass laws that are helpful to doctors. It also publishes magazines to help doctors learn about the newest kinds of medicine.

People with disabilities marched to the Capitol in 1990 to speak out for equal rights.

Interest groups often organize debates between candidates.

The second type of interest group is based on issues that concern the members. These groups try to influence the government to support their ideas. The Friends of the Earth is one such interest group. Sometimes these interest groups and ones that serve businesses have different goals. The Friends of the Earth may want to protect a certain piece of land, while the local Chamber of Commerce may want to build a mall there.

Public interest groups are the third type of group. These groups work for the interest of all people instead of serving the special interests of certain groups. The League of Women Voters is an example of a public interest group. This organization encourages every citizen to register and vote in all elections. Since the League believes that informed citizens make wise choices when voting, the group provides information about candidates from all parties before elections. It also organizes debates in which candidates can discuss their platforms.

How Do Interest Groups Influence Government?

Interest groups hire people who work to influence members of Congress and the executive branch. These professionals **lobby** government leaders in three ways. First, lobbyists bring information to members of Congress. They hope their

lobby
work to influence lawmakers

155

information will convince Congress to pass laws that are important to their interest groups. Members of Congress depend on lobbyists to inform them, since they cannot know all the information about each of the thousands of bills they must vote on.

Second, interest groups use the media to get messages about their issue to the public. Newspaper advertisements, television commercials, and television interviews with government leaders influence public opinion about different issues. Lobbyists also write letters to the public explaining the issue. Lobbyists hope that once citizens know the facts, the citizens will write or call their members of Congress to pass laws that would be helpful.

Third, lobbyists provide information to the members of their interest group about the group's goals and programs. For example, the National Education Association publishes a newspaper with information about different kinds of teaching methods, problems teachers are facing, and proposed laws to help teachers. Lobbyists hope that informed members will urge their lawmakers to support the laws they need.

Lobbyists work hard to influence Congress as well as the President and the executive departments. Lobbyists are also active in state and local governments.

Lobbyists work to influence government leaders.

Congress has passed laws to limit lobbying so that interest groups will not gain too much control over government actions. The law requires lobbyists to provide correct information about their issue to congressional committees. They can use pressure to persuade lawmakers to pass laws for their interest groups. But they cannot use force or pay lawmakers to pass certain laws.

Why Do Interest Groups Form PACs?

Interest groups want candidates to be elected who will act on their interests. To help candidates win elections, interest groups form political action committees, or PACs, that collect money for campaigns. PACs collect this money from members of their interest groups. There are now more than 4,000 PACs that contribute money to political campaigns.

Congress has limited the amount of money a PAC can contribute to a candidate's campaign fund. PACs cannot give more than $5,000 to each campaign fund, but they can contribute to many candidates. A PAC can also run its own campaign for a candidate and spend as much as it wants for their campaign. A PAC can pay for its own television commercials, newsletters, and newspaper ads to help a candidate win votes.

Do Interest Groups Help the Government?

Some people question whether or not interest groups help the nation. Some Americans believe they are harmful because certain interest groups try to pressure Congress into passing laws that are not good for the nation as a whole. Often senators and representatives feel they owe favors to PACs who contributed money to their campaign. They may pass laws to help the interest groups that supported them, even though those laws would not be the best for all people in the nation.

Other people believe interest groups are helpful to the nation. First, interest groups unite people who care about a common issue. We saw how Americans who want to stop drunk driving work together through M.A.D.D.

Second, interest groups are a source of special information for Congress. We saw that interest groups hire lobbyists who help members of Congress make decisions about bills.

discrimination
unequal treatment

Finally, interest groups help the nation by influencing the development of new laws. The special interest group called the National Organization for Women, or N.O.W., is a good example of how a special interest group can help change laws and policies. Since N.O.W. was started in 1966, laws have been passed to prevent job **discrimination** against women. Other laws require men and women to receive equal pay for doing the same job. N.O.W. has encouraged women to enter elections at all levels of government.

Interest groups play a role in all levels of government as they influence both public opinion and the work of the lawmakers. Through PACs, interest groups affect the nation's elections. While many people question whether interest groups are good or bad for the nation, everyone agrees that these groups will continue to be an important part of the American system of government.

In 1986, members of N.O.W. went to the Capitol to fight for equal rights.

Comprehension — *Write the Answer*

Write one or more sentences to answer each question.

1. What are three types of interest groups, and how do they differ from each other?

   _____

   _____

   _____

2. How are interest groups a way for citizens to be involved in government?

   _____

3. What do you think are the two most important ways lobbyists can influence

   Congress? Why? _____

   _____

4. Do you think Congress should limit lobbying? Why? _____

   _____

5. How can PACs influence elections? _____

   _____

6. Give two examples of how special interest groups have helped the nation.

   _____

   _____

Vocabulary — *Exclusions*

One word or phrase in each group does not belong. Find that word, and cross it out. Then write a sentence that tells how the other words are alike.

1. interest groups   _____
   senators
   PACs   _____
   lobbyists

2. Friends of the Earth
   League of Women Voters
   Democratic Party
   National Education Association
   _____
   _____
   _____

3. newspaper ads
   television commercials
   voter registration
   letter writing
   _____
   _____
   _____

4. discriminate
   lobby
   pressure
   influence
   _____
   _____
   _____

Critical Thinking — *Analogies*

Use a word or phrase in the box to finish each sentence. You will not use all the words.

influence	N.O.W.	wildlife
women's rights	public interest group	media
political party	PACs	

1. The American Medical Association is to a business interest group as the League of Women Voters is to a _____ .

2. Interest groups are to laws as _____ are to elections.

3. Campaign is to elect as lobby is to _____ .

4. Safe highways are to M.A.D.D. as women's rights are to _____ .

5. The American Medical Association is to doctors as Friends of the Earth is to _____ .

Skill Builder

Reviewing Line Graphs

The line graph on this page shows trends in PAC contributions to senatorial campaigns from the years 1979–80 to 1987–88. One line represents contributions to the Democrats, and the other line represents contributions to the Republicans. Study the graph and answer the questions.

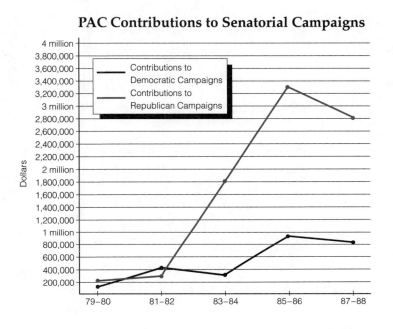

PAC Contributions to Senatorial Campaigns

1. Which party has received less PAC money in most elections? In which years did that party receive more money than the other party? _____

2. In which years did the Republicans receive the most PAC contributions to their campaigns? _____

3. In which years did the Democrats receive the most PAC contributions to their campaigns? _____

4. About how much more money did the Republicans receive than the Democrats in 1987–88? _____

5. Describe the trend between 1981–82 and 1985–86 in Republican PAC contributions.

_____

6. How would you describe the trend from 1979–80 to 1987–88 in Democratic PAC contributions? _____

FOCUS on GOVERNMENT

Senator Kassebaum's Campaign Schedule

Senator Kassebaum

In 1978, when Nancy Kassebaum became a United States Senator from Kansas, she was one of the few women elected to a full Senate term. She campaigned and was reelected in 1984 and again in 1990. The busy three-day schedule below shows how Kassebaum traveled throughout Kansas to meet as many people as possible during her campaign. Campaign managers, drivers, volunteer workers, and the Republican Party were all part of the effort to win Kassebaum's reelection to the Senate.

Senator Nancy L. Kassebaum's Schedule

Thursday, August 23, 1990

8:00 AM	Breakfast Meeting, Stan & Alta's Cafe, Chanute
9:30 AM	Tour Nu-Way Industries
10:30 AM	Depart for Iola (19 miles)
11:00 AM	Visit Iola Senior Citizens Activity Center
12:00 PM	Rotary Club Luncheon, Iola
1:30 PM	Rest and relaxation at Emerson and Mickey Lynn's home
4:00 PM	Depart for Pittsburg (70 miles)
5:30 PM	Republican Party Reception and Dinner, Pittsburg
9:00 PM	Overnight, Pittsburg

Friday, August 24, 1990

7:30 AM	Depart for Columbus (23 miles)
8:00 AM	"Breakfast with Nancy," Columbus Club, Columbus
9:30 AM	Depart for Sedan (91 miles)
12:00 PM	Luncheon, Ranch Restaurant, Sedan
1:30 PM	Visit Hills Jelly Company, Sedan
2:15 PM	Depart for Arkansas City (50 miles)
3:30 PM	Visit Presbyterian Manor, retirement and nursing home, Arkansas City
4:45 PM	Depart for Winfield (13 miles)
5:00 PM	Tour and Dinner at Cumbernaul Retirement Village, Winfield
7:00 PM	Reception, Winfield Community Center
8:30 PM	Depart for Wichita (44 miles)

Senator Kassebaum campaigning

Saturday, August 25, 1990

9:00 AM Spend day at campaign headquarters, meeting with Campaign Manager and making telephone calls

5:15 PM Depart for Phillipsburg, Spicer Flying Service, Wichita Municipal Airport

6:30 PM Drive to Logan

7:00 PM "Old Fashioned Republican Picnic," Logan

8:30 PM Return to Phillipsburg Airport and return to Topeka

Senator Kassebaum works hard for her constituents in Kansas. She met many of them during her campaign through her state.

Write About It

On a separate sheet of paper, describe three places in your neighborhood you think a candidate should visit during a campaign. Explain why you chose those three.

163

UNIT 5
Government in Action

As commander in chief of the United States, the President has the huge responsibility of protecting the nation and forming foreign policy. Police are needed to protect communities, judges are needed for our justice system, and the armed forces are needed to protect the nation. The President plans foreign policy to protect American interests in other nations. As time passes, American leaders form new foreign policies to meet the needs of a changing world. Our growing dependence on trade with foreign nations encourages our government to work peacefully with nations around the world.

Protecting our nation is a major expense that citizens share by paying taxes. Each year our nation needs a budget to pay for our foreign policy, defense needs, and hundreds of other programs. Most budget money comes from taxes. Taxpayers earn their money through a system called free enterprise, which allows people to earn and keep their profits.

In some nations there is freedom and democracy. But other governments do not allow the rights that are guaranteed by our Constitution. By studying other types of governments, Americans discover that it is worthwhile to pay taxes. The United States is a nation that protects the freedom and rights of its people.

Have You Ever Wondered . . .

- The federal government collects millions of tax dollars each year. Why doesn't the government have enough money for all of its expenses?

- The United States military has three branches. Why are three branches needed to protect the nation?

- Sweden and Saudi Arabia are two nations with kings. Why is Sweden a democracy, while Saudi Arabia is not?

All of the answers are in this unit. You will read about the many ways the government must protect the nation. You will learn about the difficult job the President faces as he plans the nation's budget. You will learn about governments in nations that are very different from our own. You will understand why we need a foreign policy that can work with different kinds of governments as events change in many parts of the world. As you read, think about the actions our government must take to meet the challenges to freedom in the United States and around the world.

165

Chapter 17

Paying for Government

Consider As You Read

- Who pays taxes and why?
- Where does tax money go?
- How are decisions about government spending made?

You have read that the government of the United States is a government "of the people, by the people, and for the people." Americans have a voice in who their leaders are and what decisions those leaders make. Americans also benefit from the protection and the many services of the government.

In this chapter, we will look at how the United States government is also "of the people." In 1989, the United States government spent over one trillion dollars. Where did this money come from? A large part of the money spent came from people who pay taxes—taxpayers.

Taxpayers and the Free Enterprise System

Taxpayers earn money through a system called free enterprise, or capitalism. In free enterprise, people have the freedom to decide how they will earn money, and they have a

People often wait in line to pay their taxes.

166

In free enterprise, people have the right to own private property.

right to earn a **profit.** All people have a right to own property and to start their own business. People can decide what kind of business to start, what **goods** to make or **services** to provide, and what prices to charge. The profits earned by a business belong to the owner. In free enterprise, almost all goods and services are provided by more than one business. So people make choices about the goods or services they will spend their money on.

In free enterprise, the government cannot tell people how to earn or spend their money. But the government protects people by being involved with the economy in four ways. First, the government spends millions of dollars each year on medical care, social security payments, and aid to the needy and people with disabilities.

Second, the government controls foreign trade. Businesses in the United States want to sell their goods to the American people. They do not want buyers to spend money on goods from other countries. Congress helps American businesses by putting taxes on goods from other countries. Then those goods are more expensive than goods made in the United States. People will then buy the cheaper goods.

Third, the government is one of the largest **consumers.** Each year it spends millions of dollars on items to help it carry out the programs that the nation needs.

Finally, the government helps consumers. Congress passes laws to protect consumers, and the laws are carried out

profit
amount earned after all bills are paid

goods
things that are made

services
things people do for others; for example, doctors, carpenters, and teachers provide services

consumers
buyers

167

through the agencies of the executive branch. For example, laws require that meat and poultry be inspected, toys pass safety tests, and medicine companies prove that their drugs help cure sickness.

How Are Our Taxes Spent?

In Units 2 and 3, you read about many jobs that the federal, the state, and the local governments do. You read on page 167 about ways the federal government protects consumers. In order to carry out these many jobs, the government needs money. Millions of dollars are spent to meet the needs of the people. Highways are built, schools are run, and police and fire fighters are hired. Printing money, protecting citizens, and cleaning up polluted lakes are a few of the hundreds of ways the government spends money.

Planning the Federal Budget

Every year, the federal government plans how it will pay for its many jobs and programs. The United States budget is enormous. Everyone, from farmers, to Cabinet secretaries, to the leader of NASA, wants part of the government's money. Not everyone gets all the money he or she wants. Planning the budget is a very difficult job. The President and his advisors must begin planning the budget at least a year before it is needed.

This woman is working to see that Congress passes laws for toy safety.

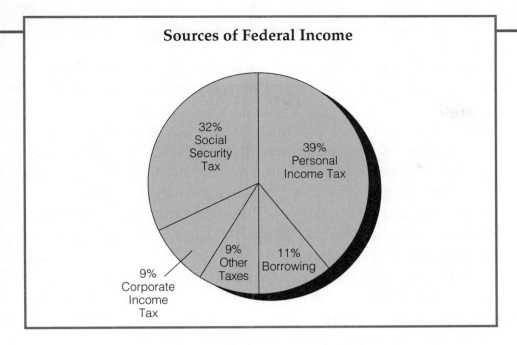

Sources of Federal Income

32% Social Security Tax

39% Personal Income Tax

9% Corporate Income Tax

9% Other Taxes

11% Borrowing

The President depends on one of the executive offices, the Office of Management and Budget (O.M.B.), for help. Budget planning begins when all executive departments and agencies send their budget needs to the O.M.B. The President and the O.M.B. use all of this information to plan how much money is needed for each executive department and agency to carry out its job.

Only Congress has the power to decide where the money actually goes. So after the President has planned a budget, it goes to Congress, where senators and representatives approve it. It is not easy to pass the budget because Congress and the President often disagree about how money should be spent. Debates in Congress and with the President will often last several months. Compromises in the budget are needed so that Congress will pass it and the President will sign it.

Taxes for the Budget

The government depends on the nation's taxpayers to pay for most of the budget. Everyone who earns **income** in the United States must pay taxes. Paying taxes is one important responsibility of all citizens.

income
money earned

Most money for the federal budget comes from three kinds of taxes. Look at the circle graph above to see how the government gets money for its budget. The circle graph shows that almost half of the money comes from personal income taxes. Personal income tax is the tax people must pay on their income. The government gets about one third of its money

169

from social security taxes. Corporate income taxes, or taxes paid by businesses, account for eleven percent of the nation's money.

State and local governments also have budgets and collect taxes to pay for their programs. Property taxes are collected by most local governments. Income tax and other kinds of taxes are collected by most states. Sales taxes are the biggest supplier of money for state and local governments. A sales tax is a tax on products sold in stores. All sales tax money is used for state and local budgets.

Many people question whether taxes are fair to all people. **Regressive taxes** like the sales tax require all people to pay the same amount of tax. Many people believe regressive taxes are unfair because people with high incomes pay the same tax as people with lower incomes. These people believe that **progressive taxes,** like the personal income tax, are much fairer. This type of tax requires people with high incomes to pay a larger portion of their income in taxes than people with lower incomes. Every year, when the budget is proposed, leaders argue about how to make taxes fair to everyone. However, no one yet feels that taxes are completely fair.

Working for a Balanced Budget

The government tries to collect enough tax money to pay all of its expenses. When the government's income is equal to all

regressive taxes
taxes that are the same amount for everyone

progressive taxes
taxes that vary depending on the ability of the person to pay

Sales taxes are taxes paid on goods we buy.

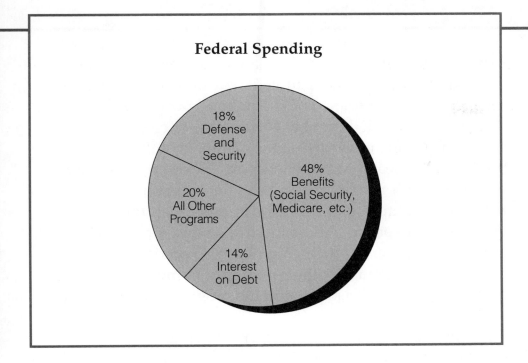

Federal Spending

- 18% Defense and Security
- 20% All Other Programs
- 14% Interest on Debt
- 48% Benefits (Social Security, Medicare, etc.)

of its budget expenses, the nation has a balanced budget. For many years, the federal budget has not been balanced. This is partly because the government has provided many services that it has not had the money to provide. So the government has chosen to borrow billions of dollars to pay for the many programs and services it provides.

The government borrows money by selling bonds to citizens and businesses. A bond is money lent to the government for a certain period of time. When that time ends, the government pays the money back plus interest. Interest is the money paid for the use of the loan. The money the government has borrowed is called the national **debt.** The national debt of the United States is now billions of dollars. The national debt grows larger as the United States continues to borrow more money. Many government leaders believe the national debt is a serious problem.

debt
money owed

To reduce the national debt, Congress passed the Budget Control Act in 1985. This law requires that all new budgets be balanced. New budgets must include plans to reduce the debt. In order to obey this law, President Bush asked Congress to raise taxes in 1990. He also found ways for departments and agencies to cut their spending.

Where Does the Money Go?

How the government spends its money depends on what the people feel is most important. In the United States, more than sixty percent of the budget goes for defense and many other kinds of benefits to people. These benefits include social security payments for senior citizens and people with disabilities, and Medicare benefits for senior citizen health care. Defense includes paying the members of the military and buying and researching new weapons. About twenty percent of the budget is used to pay interest on the national debt. The remaining eighteen percent of the budget is left for all other government expenses. These include paying for federal courts, federal prisons, post offices, highways, education, national parks, and hundreds of other programs. In most years, there is not enough money to pay for all the programs that the nation needs and wants.

All people living and working in the United States must share the responsibility of paying taxes. These taxes pay for government programs that help millions of people in every part of the nation. In this way, the United States government is also a government "of the people."

Taxes were used to pay for the shuttle Discovery.

Comprehension — *Write a Paragraph*

Use six or more words or phrases in the box to write a paragraph that explains why people in the United States must pay taxes.

highways	**trillion**	**budget**	**agencies**
income	**services**	**programs**	**taxes**
economy	**consumers**	**education**	**debt**
social security			

_____

_____

_____

_____

_____

_____

Vocabulary — *Find the Meaning*

Write the word or phrase that best completes each sentence on the blank.

1. **Capitalism** allows people to earn _____ .

    interest   pensions   profits

2. In a **free enterprise** system, people can own their own_____ .

    pets   businesses   cars

3. In free enterprise, a person can choose what **goods** their business will

    _____ .

    make   tax   earn

4. Government is a **consumer** because it _____ money on goods and services.

    saves   spends   borrows

5. **Corporate** income taxes are taxes paid by _____ .

      state   individuals   businesses

6. An example of a **regressive tax** is the _____ .

      personal income tax   corporate income tax   sales tax

7. A **progressive tax** takes more money from people with _____ .

      high incomes   low incomes   social security benefits

8. The **national debt** is money the federal government has _____ .

      borrowed   earned   saved

Critical Thinking — *Cause and Effect*

Choose a cause or an effect from **Group B** to complete each sentence in **Group A.** Write the letter of the correct answer on the blank.

Group A

1. _____ , so people must pay taxes.

2. The President cannot prepare the budget by himself, so _____ .

3. The government allows people to earn money through free enterprise, so _____ .

4. The government borrows large amounts of money to pay for the budget, so _____ .

5. The government wanted to reduce the national debt, so _____ .

6. _____ , so Congress puts taxes on many goods from other nations.

Group B

a. The Budget Control Act of 1985 requires the nation to have a balanced budget.

b. Businesses do not want consumers to buy goods from other nations.

c. The government needs money to pay for its budget.

d. The nation has a large national debt.

e. The O.M.B. helps plan the budget.

f. People have a responsibility to pay taxes on the profits they earn.

Chapter 18

Protecting the Nation

Consider As You Read
- How does the justice system protect American freedom?
- Why does the nation need a strong military?
- How do the F.B.I. and the C.I.A. protect the United States?

One of the major responsibilities of federal, state, and local governments is to protect the nation and its citizens. This protection is provided in three ways. First, our rights and freedom are protected through the justice system. Public safety is protected by the local police, and the nation's **security** is protected through the Department of Defense.

security
safety and protection

Protecting People in Their Communities

Americans depend on their local police for protection in their communities. In city budgets across the nation, paying for police protection is one of the largest expenses. Only education costs city governments more money than police protection. Millions of dollars are spent on local police forces because protecting people from crime is an important goal across the nation.

Police work in communities to protect people.

175

The Justice System Protects Our Freedom

The justice system prevents innocent people from being punished, protects the innocent from criminals, and punishes the guilty. The justice system is based on the belief that all people are innocent until they are proven guilty. To protect American freedom, the Constitution guarantees a fair trial to every accused person. If trials were not fair, people could easily be found guilty of crimes they did not commit and sentenced to harsher punishment than they deserve.

Six things are done to make sure an accused person receives a fair trial. First, the accused always has a lawyer. If people cannot afford a lawyer, the government must provide one. The accused person needs a lawyer to represent him or her in court. Second, before the trial, accused people are told what charges have been made against them. The accused has a right to know what he or she is being charged with. Third, the accused person is told about evidence that has been found for the trial. It is through the evidence that a person is proved to be innocent or guilty. Fourth, the lawyers for both the **defense** and the **prosecution** must obey the same rules in court. The judge cannot favor either side during a trial. Fifth, the trial must be open to the public. A fair trial cannot be held secretly. Sixth, the trial must be decided by an **impartial** jury. Jury members cannot believe that the accused person is guilty before the trial begins. They cannot know anything about the case or have heard about it in the media.

defense
side that tries to prove that the accused person is innocent

prosecution
side that tries to prove that the accused person is guilty

impartial
fair; not taking sides

An accused person has the right to have a lawyer.

176

The F.B.I. entered this building to find clues in a bombing case.

Every American citizen has the right to a fair jury trial. It is also the responsibility of every citizen to serve on a jury if called to do so. During a trial, the jury hears evidence about the accused person. Then the members of the jury decide on a **verdict.** If the jury finds the accused person guilty, it is the responsibility of either the judge, that jury, or a new jury to decide on the punishment for the guilty person.

verdict
the decision of a jury

The Federal Bureau of Investigation

The F.B.I., or the Federal Bureau of Investigation, helps both the local police and the justice system. This agency is part of the executive branch's Department of Justice. The main goal of the F.B.I. is to find facts and evidence for cases that involve the federal government. The F.B.I. finds witnesses to crimes and provides information about fingerprints to help local officers locate missing criminals.

The Department of Defense Protects the Nation

The Department of Defense is in charge of all American military forces. It is responsible for protecting national security. This means protecting the United States from attack and making it safe for Americans and American businesses in other parts of the world. The main offices of the Department of Defense are in the huge Pentagon building near Washington, D.C.

The Framers of the Constitution knew that the military had a lot of power. They were careful to check the power of the military with civilian power. The President is commander in chief of the armed forces, and Congress decides how much money the military gets.

The highest military position in the nation is the Chairperson of the Joint Chiefs of Staff. The other Joint Chiefs of Staff are the highest officers of the Army, Navy, Air Force, and Marines. The Joint Chiefs of Staff advise the President, the Secretary of Defense, and the National Security Council on the nation's security needs.

The National Security Council was created by Congress to help the President plan defense and foreign policies. The National Security Council is part of the Executive Office. People from the Department of Defense work with the National Security Council to advise the President on American security in every part of the world.

The Branches of the Military

The Department of the Army is the largest branch of the military. Members of the Army are trained to fight on land. The Army includes the National Guard. These soldiers are trained to help their states during emergencies such as floods, earthquakes, and riots.

The Army is one branch of the military.

The Department of the Navy protects American interests at sea. Naval ships are used to transport soldiers, supplies, weapons, and airplanes to battle regions. Although the Marines are part of the Department of the Navy, they have their own directors. The Marines fight on land for the Navy.

The Department of the Air Force provides pilots and planes for the nation's defense. The Air Force is now the first line of defense during a war. This means that during a war, the Air Force weakens the enemy by bombing its weapons and supplies. After the Air Force has weakened the enemy, the Army sends its soldiers into battle to win the war on the ground.

All members of the three military branches are volunteers. Although all men must register for the draft when they are eighteen years old, at this time only volunteers serve in the armed forces. Many women serve in all branches, and they are trained for **combat.**

The Pentagon

combat
fighting

Other Agencies Protect American Security

Congress also created the Central Intelligence Agency, the C.I.A., to collect **intelligence** about other nations. Intelligence information is used to make military and foreign policy decisions. Although much of the C.I.A.'s information comes from foreign newspapers and television programs, the C.I.A. also depends on spies to obtain intelligence information. To protect information about American security from being known in other parts of the world, all C.I.A. work is done secretly. Not even Congress or the President knows everything about the C.I.A.'s work.

intelligence
information

American Freedom Depends on National Security

The United States must have a strong defense system to protect its security and independence. If another nation ever won control of the United States, the Constitution could no longer be the law of the nation. If this happened, Americans everywhere could lose their rights and their freedom. Only through good police protection, a fair justice system, and a strong defense system can the nation protect its independence and the freedom of its people.

Using What You Learned

Comprehension — *Reviewing the Important Facts*

Match the sentence in **Group A** with the word or phrase from **Group B** that the sentence explains. Write the letter of the correct answer on the blank.

Group A

_____ 1. These soldiers can be called to help with state emergencies.

_____ 2. At the end of a trial, all of these people must reach a verdict.

_____ 3. These people try to prove that an accused person is innocent.

_____ 4. These people fight on land for the Navy.

_____ 5. This agency works secretly to collect intelligence.

_____ 6. This department is in charge of all the military forces.

_____ 7. This bureau provides information to local police.

_____ 8. This agency advises the President on American security.

Group B

a. Department of Defense

b. F.B.I.

c. Marines

d. C.I.A.

e. National Guard

f. defense

g. National Security Council

h. jury

Vocabulary — *Writing With Vocabulary*

Use six or more words in the box to write a paragraph that explains three ways that the government protects the nation.

civilian	intelligence	security
combat	verdict	defense
prosecution	armed forces	justice
trial	lawyer	military

_____

_____

_____

_____

_____

_____

Critical Thinking — *Categories*

Read the words in each group. Decide how they are alike. Write a title for each group on the blank beside each group. You may use the words in the box for all or part of each title.

National Security Council	trial	C.I.A.
Air Force	F.B.I.	military

1. lawyer
   impartial jury
   public

   _____

2. find evidence
   locate witnesses
   collect fingerprints

   _____

3. advises on foreign policy
   advises on national security
   works with Department of Defense

   _____

4. Department of the Army
   Department of the Navy
   Department of the Air Force

   _____

5. pilots
   planes
   first line of defense

   _____

6. intelligence
   spies
   secret

   _____

Chapter 19

Other Forms of Government

Consider As You Read
- What other forms of government are there?
- How can democracy be different in other nations?
- What kind of government is ruled by a king?

The Constitution of the United States is a plan for a government ruled by the people. Can a nation be a democracy without a president and without the separation of powers? Are there governments in the world today that rule without free elections? Are there governments that do not allow personal freedom? The answer is yes to all of these questions. In this chapter we will study three different kinds of government found in the world today.

Sweden: A Different Kind of Democracy

Sweden is a democracy in northern Europe. Sweden's government differs from American democracy in three important ways. First, Sweden is a constitutional **monarchy.** In

monarchy
rule by a king or queen

Sweden is a monarchy. It has a king and a queen.

182

Stockholm is the capital of Sweden.

a constitutional monarchy, the king or queen has only those powers that are allowed by the nation's constitution. The prime minister is the real leader of Sweden's government. Sweden's king attends ceremonies and acts as a symbol of the nation, but the king has no power to rule or make laws. Great Britain and the Netherlands are other democracies with constitutional monarchies.

The second difference between Swedish and American governments is that Sweden has a parliament. Swedes vote in free elections for representatives to make laws for them in parliament. The leader of the majority party in the parliament is Sweden's prime minister. Important parliament members are chosen to be cabinet ministers. About twenty ministers help the prime minister carry out the laws made by parliament. The prime minister is part of both the executive and legislative branches. Although there is no separation of powers between the executive and legislative branches in a parliamentary democracy, freedom is protected by the Swedish constitution. Parliamentary democracies are also found in Great Britain, Canada, Japan, and other nations.

The third difference between American and Swedish governments is that Sweden has a multiparty system. Unlike the United States, which has just two major political parties, Sweden has five. Although the five parties have representatives in the parliament, the Socialist Party has been the majority party for more than fifty years.

Socialism and the Swedish Government

The economic system in Sweden is based on socialism. It is not like American free enterprise. Socialism is also found in other democracies such as Great Britain, Denmark, and Israel.

A socialist economy has four features. First, it has **welfare** programs to help everyone in the nation. The government provides many kinds of benefits to every age group. Parents are paid allowances for every child in their family so they can buy what their children need. People who lose their jobs are paid until they find work. All retired people are paid excellent pensions. Every worker receives four weeks of paid vacation each year. There is free health care for everyone.

The millions of dollars needed for the many benefits come from Swedish taxpayers. Taxes are much higher in Sweden than in most nations. Most Swedes believe it is worth paying high taxes when they receive so many benefits.

The second feature of a socialist economy is that the government owns and controls some of the major businesses. The Swedish government controls iron mines, water power plants, television stations, and the railroads. Third, the government allows people to own their own businesses. In Sweden, most factories, farms, and stores are privately owned. Fourth, the government sets goals for farming and manufacturing.

welfare
help for the needy

The government of Sweden provides education for everyone.

184

Saudi Arabia: Another Kind of Monarchy

Although Saudi Arabia has a king like Sweden does, its government is very different from Sweden's. Saudi Arabia is an absolute monarchy in which the king has almost complete power. There is no constitution in Saudi Arabia to limit the king's power. In an absolute monarchy, the king has legislative, executive, and judicial powers.

The King of Saudi Arabia

In Saudi Arabia, the king is also an important leader of Islam, the nation's religion. The nation is ruled by the laws of Islam. All people in Saudi Arabia must follow Islam.

The government in Saudi Arabia is controlled by the royal family. It is a huge family with several thousand members. A group of important family members picks one man from the royal family to be the nation's king. The religious leaders approve of the family's choice. Then the new king appoints a group of men to advise him. These advisors are always chosen from the royal family.

Saudi Arabia's absolute monarchy limits the freedom of its people. Free elections are not allowed. Freedom of the press, freedom of speech, and freedom of assembly are not allowed. The king acts as the nation's Supreme Court. He can use his judicial powers to interpret the religious laws for his own interests.

Unlike Sweden and the United States, religion plays a very important role in the government of Saudi Arabia. One major job of the Saudi government is to make sure everyone follows the laws of Islam. The nation has religion police who find and punish people who do not follow Islam. For example, the law requires women to cover their faces and bodies with long, black veils when they are in the street. When the police find women who do not obey these laws, the women are punished. All court decisions are based on religious laws. Many people who are not Muslims have come from other nations to work in Saudi Arabia. These people are not allowed to practice their own religions.

China Has a Communist Economy

In 1949, a revolution in China put the Communist Party in charge of the government. Before the revolution, millions of people were poor and hungry. A few wealthy people owned

185

the land and factories, but they did not care about their workers. So the workers did not work very hard. Farms were not producing many crops, and factories were also doing badly. There was almost no trade between China and other nations. A change was needed.

The Communist Party took control. It tried to stop hunger and improve production. It divided the land into farms that were owned and run by the government. Since the 1970s, the government has allowed free enterprise. Many people now own small businesses. Although all farmland is owned by the government, farmers now have **production contracts** with the government. After farmers grow the required amount of food for the government, they can sell the **surplus** and keep the profits. Since farmers can earn money by growing more food, they work harder, and food production has increased. Hunger is no longer a problem in China.

production contracts
agreements to produce a certain amount

surplus
extra

China: An Authoritarian Government

The government of China, like the government of Saudi Arabia, limits the freedom of its people. China has an authoritarian government. Almost every area of life is controlled by the government.

China's government includes a People's Congress and a president, but the nation is ruled by the Chinese Communist Party. The general secretary of the Communist Party is the most powerful person in China. Party members control local governments, but they have no influence on the major decisions of the Communist Party.

The army of China helps carry out the policies of the Communist Party. When necessary, the army uses force to make people obey party policies.

In 1949, communist soldiers fought to gain control of China's government.

In May 1989, thousands of students spoke out against the government in China.

The Communist Party and Chinese Life

The authoritarian government in China allows little personal freedom. Freedom of speech, religion, and the press are not allowed. People cannot move from one part of China to another without permission from the government. The government directs all education programs in order to control how people think about their nation.

The Communist Party does not allow people to demonstrate against the government. When people try to speak out to change the government, they are punished. This happened in 1989 when thousands of Chinese students demonstrated for more freedom in Tiananmen Square in the city of Beijing. When the students refused to stop their demonstrations, the army was sent to attack them. Many students were killed by the army, and the demonstrations ended.

Throughout the world, there are different types of governments. After World War II, communist governments took control of many nations in Europe, but many of those nations are now moving away from communism. Today there are only a few absolute monarchies, but many nations are ruled by leaders who permit little personal freedom. By comparing American democracy to other types of government, we can appreciate the freedoms that are guaranteed by our Constitution.

Using What You Learned

Comprehension — *Finish the Paragraph*

Use the words in the box to finish the paragraph. Write the words you choose on the correct blanks.

revolution	parliamentary	government	royal
personal	speech	welfare	
socialist	communist	Communist Party	

Sweden is a _____ democracy with a _____

economy. The government provides _____ programs to help people.

China became a _____ nation after a _____

in 1949. After that, all farms and factories were owned by the _____.

China is ruled by the _____ . The government allows little

_____ freedom. Saudi Arabia, like China, does not allow freedom of

religion , of the press, or of _____ . The king has full power to rule

with his _____ family.

Vocabulary — *Exclusions*

One word or phrase in each group does not belong. Find that word and cross it out. Then write a sentence that tells how the other words are alike.

1. authoritarian government
   constitutional monarchy
   parliamentary democracy
   free enterprise

   _____

   _____

   _____

2. royal family
   absolute monarchy
   freedom of religion
   no constitution

   _____

   _____

   _____

3. The United States
   Great Britain
   Sweden
   China

   _____

   _____

   _____

4. authoritarian government
   freedom of speech
   production contracts
   communist economy

   _____

   _____

   _____

5. paid vacations
   allowances for children
   low taxes
   free health care

   _____

   _____

   _____

Critical Thinking — *Fact or Opinion*

Read each sentence below. If the sentence is a fact, write **F** on the blank. If the sentence is an opinion, write **O** on the blank. If the sentence gives both a fact and an opinion, write **FO** on the blank, and circle the part of the sentence that is an opinion.

_____ 1. Sweden is a constitutional monarchy, and its king has little power.

_____ 2. American democracy with its separation of powers is better than parliamentary democracy.

_____ 3. People in Sweden pay high taxes, but it is worth paying high taxes to get the benefits.

_____ 4. There are five major political parties in Sweden.

_____ 5. In Saudi Arabia, religion police enforce the laws of Islam.

_____ 6. It is unfair that Saudi women should have to wear veils.

_____ 7. People who are not Muslims should not live in Saudi Arabia.

_____ 8. China is an authoritarian government, because the Communist Party has great control over every area of life.

_____ 9. Chinese students protested for freedom at Tiananmen Square in 1989, and the government should have listened to the demands of the students.

Skill Builder

Reading a Chart

We read charts to learn facts quickly. Read the chart below. Then answer each question.

The Governments of China, Saudi Arabia, and Sweden			
	China	Saudi Arabia	Sweden
Population	1,200,000,000	18,200,000	8,800,000
Type of Economy	Communist	Free Enterprise	Socialist
Type of Government	Authoritarian	Absolute Monarchy	Constitutional Monarchy
Government Leadership	Communist Party-controlled state	King	Prime Minister
Free Elections	No	No	Yes
Criticism of Government	Not Allowed	Not Allowed	Allowed
Freedom of Speech, Press, Religion	Not Allowed	Not Allowed	Allowed
Average Personal Yearly Income	$360	$9,000	$16,900
Political Parties	One	None	Five

1. Compare the populations of the three nations.

   _____

2. What kinds of economies are found in China, Saudi Arabia, and Sweden?

   _____

3. In which nation is the average personal yearly income the smallest?

   _____

4. Explain two ways the governments of Saudi Arabia and China are the same.

   _____

5. Explain two ways China and Saudi Arabia differ.

   _____

Chapter 20

In the Global Community

Consider As You Read

- Why is American foreign policy always changing?
- What are the important foreign policy goals of the United States?
- How does the United States carry out its foreign policies?

invasion
one nation's army entering another nation by force

In August 1990, the president of Iraq led his army into Kuwait, a small, oil-rich nation that shares a border with Iraq. Leaders around the world spoke out against the **invasion.** The world reacted strongly to the invasion for two reasons. First, people felt that Iraq had no right to invade Kuwait. Second, many nations around the world depend on the oil from nations in the Middle East. Leaders wanted to protect their nations' interest in oil from this area, including Kuwait.

One of these leaders was President George Bush. He and leaders from several other nations worked together to force Iraq to leave Kuwait. Protecting the interests of the United States and helping other nations defend themselves from invasion are two goals of American foreign policy.

Soldiers from many nations fought together to force the army of Iraq out of Kuwait.

What Is American Foreign Policy?

interdependence
depending on one another

American foreign policy is the action the United States takes in dealing with other nations. Foreign policy is important because of growing **interdependence** among the nations of the world. The United States depends on other nations for natural resources and goods of many kinds. Through foreign policy, the United States works with other nations to promote trade and peace.

Since the United States became a nation, American leaders have planned foreign policies to meet the nation's needs. Some of our foreign-policy goals, such as protecting our freedom of the seas, have remained the same. Other goals have changed. Foreign-policy goals often promote American self-interest. For example, since the end of World War II, one of our foreign-policy goals has been to achieve peace in the Middle East. One reason for this goal is that the United States depends on oil from the Middle East for its cars, planes, and factories. If there is a **conflict** there, our supply of oil might be threatened.

conflict
fight, disagreement, or war

The United States now has four major foreign-policy goals. The first goal is to protect the security of Americans and American businesses in all parts of the world. The second goal is to improve our economy by having better trade with other nations. Since the United States does not have all the resources it needs, and American businesses cannot provide all the goods and services Americans need, we depend on other

Nations depend on one another for resources and goods.

During a great battle in World War II, thousands of American troops landed on the beaches of France.

nations for their resources and products. Third, the United States wants to promote world peace. So the United States has signed treaties with many nations. The fourth goal is to promote democracy, independence, and **human rights** in other nations. The United States wants all nations to respect the human rights of citizens. It does not want nations taking control of other nations.

human rights
basic rights of all people

How Has American Foreign Policy Changed?

George Washington, our first President, encouraged the United States to have a foreign policy of **isolationism.** Washington believed the United States did not have a strong enough army to become involved in conflicts with other nations. Then in 1823, President Monroe developed the Monroe Doctrine, which became the new American foreign policy. The Monroe Doctrine said that the Western Hemisphere would be controlled by the people of North and South America and not by European nations.

isolationism
staying separate from others

After World War I, the United States returned to a policy of isolationism. Americans hoped to avoid fighting in future wars by avoiding conflicts with other nations. Our policy of isolationism ended when Japan attacked a military base on the island of Hawaii during World War II. The United States fought with other nations to win the war, and then helped work out the peace treaties after World War II. By the end of World War II, the United States had become a superpower.

After World War II, Communist governments began to take control of the nations of Eastern Europe. The United States did not want communism to spread throughout the world. The United States began a new policy to keep communism from spreading. This was called the Cold War. The Cold War was a war of words and ideas. It was mainly between the United States and the other superpower, the Soviet Union. The Cold War lasted almost 40 years. In the late 1980s, the Communist governments in Eastern Europe changed into democracies. The Cold War finally ended in 1991 when the Soviet Union broke apart into 15 separate countries. The Communist government ended there, too.

The United States forms new foreign policies as relations change between the United States and other nations. In recent years the United States has been more involved in working for peace in many countries.

Who Carries Out American Foreign Policy?

One of the major responsibilities of the President is to make and carry out foreign policy. The President can sign treaties, negotiate agreements, and send troops into action in any part of the world. The President makes his decisions with advice

In December 1989, President Bush and President Gorbachev of the Soviet Union met to negotiate an agreement.

from the National Security Council and the Department of State.

Congress also plays a role in American foreign policy. All treaties and appointments of ambassadors require Senate approval. Only Congress can appropriate the money needed for defense and for foreign aid to help other nations. A President can decide to go to war against another nation, but only Congress can declare war.

The Department of State, one of the executive departments, advises the President on foreign policy. It is responsible for embassies and ambassadors that work for American interests in foreign nations.

The United States uses these six methods to carry out its foreign policy:

1. Treaties—The United States has defense treaties with about fifty nations. Defense treaties allow the United States to use military force to defend other nations. These treaties protect American interests abroad and foreign nations from attack. Other treaties promote peace. In 1987, the United States and the Soviet Union signed the I.N.F. Treaty. With this treaty both nations agreed to destroy a large number of nuclear weapons.

2. Alliances—Alliances are agreements between the United States and other nations to help each other for economic or military reasons. Alliances are made formal when the nations sign treaties. The North Atlantic Treaty Organization, N.A.T.O., is a military alliance between the United States, Canada, and fourteen European nations. All of the nations of N.A.T.O. have agreed to defend each other during a war.

Peace Corps Volunteers

3. Military Force—The United States can send troops to fight in any part of the world. In 1990, President Bush sent American military forces to Saudi Arabia to fight with other nations against Iraq.

4. Peace Corps—The Peace Corps was started by President Kennedy in 1961. It sends American volunteers to developing nations where they live and work with those nations' people. Peace Corps members work with people to improve health care, agriculture, and education.

5. Negotiations—Negotiations can be used to settle problems between nations and to decide how much **foreign aid** the United States will give other nations. In 1979,

foreign aid
money, food, and medicine for other nations

195

President Carter helped Israel and Egypt agree to end their long conflict and sign a peace treaty.

6. The United Nations—The United States is a member of the United Nations. It works to maintain peace throughout the world.

The United Nations and American Foreign Policy

At the end of World War II, many nations formed an organization to help nations solve problems peacefully. The United States became one of the United Nation's first members in 1945. The United Nations now has 184 member nations.

Members of the United Nations meet at the annual General Assembly meetings. Problems relating to world peace are discussed. Sometimes, members pass a resolution about the best way to solve a problem. The resolution sends a strong message. However, the General Assembly cannot force nations to follow the resolutions.

The Security Council of the United Nations has the power to carry out resolutions. The Security Council has five permanent members and ten members who serve for two-year terms. The United States is one of the permanent members. The permanent members have the power to veto Security Council resolutions.

The Security Council of the United Nations met in September 1990 to discuss the attack on Kuwait by Iraq.

Many world leaders, such as President Bill Clinton, give speeches at the annual meeting of the General Assembly.

The United States depends on the United Nations to carry out some of its foreign policies. It was through the Security Council that the United States took action against Iraq's attack on Kuwait. First, the Security Council passed **economic sanctions** against Iraq. Because of these sanctions, most nations stopped trading with Iraq. Since the Security Council agreed that military force could be used to make Iraq leave Kuwait, the United States joined other nations in a war against Iraq. In February 1991, Iraq left Kuwait.

economic sanctions
limits to trade

The Challenges of Foreign Policy

The Persian Gulf War is a good example of the interdependence of the United States with the rest of the world. Many nations responded when Iraq invaded Kuwait, and many nations worked together to force Iraq to leave.

In the 1990s, energy shortages, growing environmental problems, and the danger of nuclear weapons are a few of the challenges American leaders must face as they plan new foreign policies. The challenge of bringing peace to troubled regions like the Middle East remains part of American foreign policy. Protecting human rights abroad and constitutional freedom for all Americans are also very important to foreign-policy makers. Through foreign policy, the United States is connected to the other nations of the world.

Using What You Learned

Comprehension — *Who Said It?*

Read each statement. Then look in the box for the person who might have said it. Write the name of the person you choose on the blank after each sentence.

Peace Corps volunteer **soldier**	**Secretary of State** **George Washington**	**member of Congress** **President Monroe**

1. "I believe isolationism is the best foreign policy for the United States, since we do

   not have a strong army and navy." _____

2. "My foreign policy is that the Western Hemisphere must be controlled only by people in North and South America. The United States will not allow Europe to

   control this hemisphere." _____

3. "I must advise the President about foreign policy." _____

4. "I will vote for the United States to give more foreign aid to Latin America."

   _____

5. "I will work with people in a developing nation for two years, and I will help them

   learn modern farming and health care." _____

6. "I will fight for the United States if we go to war." _____

Vocabulary — *Choosing Vocabulary*

Choose a word or phrase from the box to complete each sentence. Write that word or phrase on the blank.

foreign aid **interdependence** **alliance**	**conflicts** **invasion** **human rights**	**economic sanctions** **superpower**

1. Many people did not approve of the _____ of Kuwait by Iraq.

2. The rights that should belong to all people in the world are called

   _____ .

3. Foreign policy is used to avoid _____ with other nations.

4. A nation that is more powerful than most nations is called a

   _____ .

5. Because of the _____ with other nations, it is important for the
   United States to work for peace around the world.

6. The United States gives _____ to other nations in the form of
   money, food, and medicine.

7. An _____ is an agreement between nations that agree to help
   each other.

8. When the Security Council asked nations not to buy or sell products from Iraq, it

   wanted _____ to force Iraq to leave Kuwait.

Critical Thinking — *Distinguishing Relevant Information*

Imagine that you have to tell a friend why foreign policy is needed to protect American self-interest. Read each sentence below. Decide which sentences are relevant to what you will say. Put a check in front of the relevant sentences.

_____ 1. The United States needs resources from other nations.

_____ 2. The United States is part of the United Nations.

_____ 3. The Cold War started after World War II ended.

_____ 4. The United States trades with many nations around the world.

_____ 5. Many Americans live in other nations.

_____ 6. The United States has a large military.

_____ 7. Americans buy many goods from other nations.

_____ 8. The United States once had a policy of isolationism.

Skill Builder

Reading a Political Cartoon

The political cartoon below is about the Persian Gulf War. The man with "Iraq" on his sleeve is Saddam Hussein, leader of Iraq. Study the cartoon. Then answer the questions.

1. What are the two men on the left doing? _____

   _____

2. What action does that part of the cartoon stand for? _____

   _____

3. Who is talking? _____

4. The words *deplorable, reprehensible, repulsive,* and *despicable* all mean terrible or awful.

   What do they refer to? _____

   _____

5. Why are the Arabs holding George Bush's hand? _____

   _____

6. Why would the one Arab be happy that oil prices are going up? _____

   _____

7. What do you think the cartoonist's opinion of the United Nations' involvement in

   the Persian Gulf is? _____

   _____

Jimmy Carter (1924–)

Jimmy Carter

Jimmy Carter was President of the United States from 1977 to 1981. While he was President, he worked for peace and human rights at home and around the world. After his presidency, his work did not stop.

As President, Carter spoke out strongly against nations that abused the human rights of their people. He criticized nations that put citizens in jail just because they had spoken against their government. He limited American trade with nations that abused human rights.

Carter helped Israel and Egypt negotiate a peace treaty. Egypt had been in a state of war with Israel for more than thirty years. In 1978, Carter brought the leaders of Israel and Egypt together. He helped them find ways that their countries could begin living at peace with one another.

At home in the United States, President Carter worked for equal rights and to end poverty. He created almost 8 million jobs, and he cut some of the national debt. He appointed more women and minorities to positions in the government than any other President before him.

Today Carter continues to work for some of the same things he did as President. He and his wife write many letters and make many phone calls to leaders of other nations. They ask that people who are in jail for speaking against the government be freed. They have helped save several lives and get hundreds of people out of jail.

He has helped nations in Latin America run fair and free elections. He has traveled to Africa to help leaders of nations that are at war find peace.

Building Houses

In the United States, Carter fights poverty. He started a group, Habitat for Humanity, to build houses for people who are homeless. Volunteers in communities give their time and skills to build the houses. Hundreds of homeless people in the United States now have places to live.

Jimmy Carter has helped many people around the world in many ways. He knows it is important to be a citizen of the world as well as of the nation.

The Inauguration Speech of President John F. Kennedy

John F. Kennedy

John F. Kennedy became the thirty-fifth President of the United States on January 20, 1961. What follows is part of the speech he gave on that day, after he took the oath of office. Nuclear weapons were fairly new, and many people, including Kennedy, were concerned about their possible use.

Let the word go forth . . . that the torch has been passed to a new generation of Americans . . . unwilling to witness or permit the slow undoing of those human rights to which this nation has always been committed and to which we are committed today at home and around the world.

Let every nation know, whether it wishes us well or ill, that we shall pay any price, bear any burden, meet any hardship, support any friend, oppose any **foe,** to assure the survival and the success of liberty. . . .

To those old **allies** . . . we pledge the loyalty of faithful friends. . . .

To those new states whom we welcome to the ranks of the free, we . . . hope to find them strongly supporting their own freedom. . . .

To those peoples in the huts and villages of half the globe struggling to break the bonds of mass **misery,** we **pledge** our best efforts to help them help themselves. . . . If a free society cannot help the many who are poor, it cannot save the few who are rich. . . .

To . . . the United Nations, our last best hope in an age where the instruments of war have far outpaced the instruments of peace, we renew our pledge of support. . . .

Finally, to those nations who would make themselves our **adversary,** we offer . . . a request: that both sides begin anew the **quest** for peace. . . .

So let us begin anew. . . . Let us never negotiate out of fear. But let us never fear to negotiate.

Let both sides seek to **invoke** the wonders of science instead

foe
enemy

allies
friends

misery
unhappiness or pain

pledge
promise

adversary
enemy

quest
search

invoke
call upon

of its terrors. Together let us explore the stars, conquer the deserts, **eradicate** disease, tap the ocean depths, and encourage the arts and commerce. . . .

eradicate
end

Let both sides join in creating . . . a new world of law, where the strong are just and the weak secure and the peace preserved.

All this will not be finished in the first one hundred days. Nor will it be finished in the first one thousand days, nor in the life of this administration, nor even perhaps in our lifetime on this planet. But let us begin.

And so, my fellow Americans: ask not what your country can do for you—ask what you can do for your country.

My fellow citizens of the world: ask not what America will do for you, but what together we can do for the freedom of man.

Write About It

Write a paragraph that tells what you, as a citizen of the United States, can do for your country. Be as specific as possible.

Kennedy gave his speech on January 20, 1961.

203

The Declaration of Independence

When in the course of human events, it becomes necessary for one people to dissolve the political bands which have connected them with another, and to assume among the powers of the earth the separate and equal station to which the laws of nature and of nature's God entitle them, a decent respect to the opinions of mankind requires that they should declare the causes which impel them to the separation.

Sometimes in history, one group of people must become independent from the nation that rules it. The people who are breaking ties must then explain their reasons to the world. That is the purpose of this Declaration of Independence.

We hold these truths to be self-evident: that all men are created equal, that they are endowed by their Creator with certain unalienable rights, that among these are life, liberty, and the pursuit of happiness.

We believe the following things are always true. All people are equal. God gave all people the natural rights of life, liberty, and working for happiness.

That to secure these rights, governments are instituted among men, deriving their just powers from the consent of the governed; that whenever any form of government becomes destructive of these ends, it is the right of the people to alter or to abolish it, and to institute new government, laying its foundation on such principles and organizing its powers in such form as to them shall seem most likely to effect their safety and happiness. Prudence, indeed, will dictate that governments long established should not be changed for light and transient causes; and accordingly all experience has shown, that mankind are more disposed to suffer while evils are sufferable, than to right themselves by abolishing the forms to which they are accustomed. But when a long train of abuses and usurpations, pursuing invariably the same object, evinces a design to reduce them under absolute despotism, it is their right, it is their duty, to throw off such government, and to provide new guards for their future security.

Governments are created by people to protect the people's rights. Governments get their power by the consent of the people they rule. People have the right to change or end a government that takes away their natural rights. The people must then start a new government that will protect natural rights. People should never revolt for only a few, unimportant reasons. However, when there is a long history of repeated abuses, then it is the right and the duty of the people to overthrow the ruling government and start a new government that will safeguard the rights of all people.

Such has been the patient sufferance of these colonies; and such is now the necessity which constrains them to alter their former systems of government. The history of the present king of Great Britain is a history of repeated injuries and usurpations, all having in direct object the establishment of an absolute tyranny over these states. To prove this, let facts be submitted to a candid world.

For a long time, the colonies have suffered abuses from the king's government, and so we must change our government. King George, through many unfair actions, has shown that his goals are to take away our rights and to have complete control over the colonies. We want the world to know the following facts about the king's abuses:

He has refused his assent to laws, the most wholesome and necessary for the public good.

The king has refused to approve laws necessary for the good of the colonies.

He has forbidden his governors to pass laws of immediate and pressing importance, unless suspended in their operation till his assent should be obtained, and when so suspended, he has utterly neglected to attend to them.

He has not allowed laws to be passed without his approval. And he has taken a long time to approve those he allows.

He has refused to pass other laws for the accommodation of large districts of people, unless those people would relinquish the right of representation in the legislature, a right inestimable to them and formidable to tyrants only.

He has not allowed all people to have equal representation in the legislatures.

He has called together legislative bodies at places unusual, uncomfortable, and distant from the depository of their public records, for the sole purpose of fatiguing them into compliance with his measures.

He has forced representatives to meet in strange, uncomfortable, and far-off places in order to make them so tired that they would obey his orders.

He has dissolved Representative Houses repeatedly, for opposing with manly firmness his invasions on the rights of the people.

He has shut down colonial legislatures many times when they criticized the king's abuses of the people.

He has refused, for a long time after such dissolutions, to cause others to be elected; whereby the legislative powers, incapable of annihilation, have returned to the people at large for their exercise; the state remaining, in the mean time, exposed to all the dangers of invasion from without and convulsions within.

After shutting down legislatures, he has taken a long time before holding new elections. The people were in danger because their colonial governments could not make laws to protect them.

He has endeavored to prevent the population of these states; for that purpose obstructing the laws of naturalization of foreigners, refusing to pass others to encourage their migration hither, and raising the conditions of new appropriations of lands.

King George has tried to stop the colonial population from growing by making it difficult for Europeans to come to the colonies. He has made it difficult to buy land in America.

He has obstructed the administration of justice, by refusing his assent to laws for establishing judiciary powers.

He stopped us from carrying out justice by refusing to let us set up courts.

He has made judges dependent on his will alone, for the tenure of their offices, and the amount and payment of their salaries.

Judges depend on the king for their salaries and their jobs, so they make unfair decisions to keep their jobs.

He has erected a multitude of new offices and sent hither swarms of officers to harass our people, and eat out their substance.

The king sent large numbers of people from Britain to control us, bother us, and use up our resources.

He has kept among us, in times of peace,

standing armies without the consent of our legislatures.

Even in peaceful times, the king has kept his armies in the colonies without the consent of our legislatures.

He has affected to render the military independent of and superior to the civil power.

He has tried to make the military free from, and more powerful than, our government.

He has combined with others to subject us to a jurisdiction foreign to our constitution, and unacknowledged by our laws, giving his assent to their acts of pretended legislation:

King George has worked with Parliament to give us these unfair laws that we did not help write:

For quartering large bodies of armed troops among us;

They forced us to allow British soldiers to stay in our homes.

For protecting them, by a mock trial, from punishment for any murders which they should commit on the inhabitants of these states;

They protected soldiers who murdered our people by giving them fake trials.

For cutting off our trade with all parts of the world;

They stopped us from trading with other nations.

For imposing taxes on us without our consent;

They made unfair tax laws for us.

For depriving us, in many cases, of the benefits of trial by jury;

They often took away our right to have fair jury trials.

For transporting us beyond seas, to be tried for pretended offenses;

They forced some of our people to travel to Britain to go on trial for crimes they never committed.

For abolishing the free system of English laws in a neighboring province, establishing therein an arbitrary government and enlarging its boundaries so as to render it at once an example and fit instrument for introducing the same absolute rule into these colonies;

They took away Quebec's fair government and gave Quebec an unfair government. They can use Quebec as an example of how to bring absolute government to the colonies.

For taking away our charters, abolishing our most valuable laws, and altering fundamentally the forms of our governments;

They took away our charters, they changed our most important laws, and they changed the kind of government we have.

For suspending our own legislatures, and declaring themselves invested with power to legislate for us in all cases whatsoever.

They have stopped us from meeting in our legislatures. They say they have the power to make all laws for us.

He has abdicated government here, by declaring us out of his protection and waging war against us.

King George has given up his power to rule us since he says he cannot protect us and is now fighting a war against us.

He has plundered our seas, ravaged our coasts, burnt our towns, and destroyed the lives of our people.

The king has attacked our ships, destroyed our ports, burned our towns, and destroyed our lives.

He is at this time transporting large armies of foreign mercenaries to complete the works of death, desolation, and tyranny already begun with circumstances of cruelty and perfidy scarcely paralleled in the most barbarous ages, and totally unworthy the head of a civilized nation.

He is bringing foreign armies to kill us and destroy the colonies. These soldiers show cruelty that should not be allowed by a modern king.

He has constrained our fellow citizens, taken captive on the high seas, to bear arms against their country, to become the executioners of their friends and brethren, or to fall themselves by their hands.

He has taken Americans off our ships at sea and has forced them to fight against their own people.

He has excited domestic insurrections amongst us, and has endeavored to bring on the inhabitants of our frontiers the merciless Indian savages, whose known rule of warfare, is an undistinguished destruction of all ages, sexes and conditions.

He has told our slaves and servants to fight against us, and he has encouraged the Indians to attack us.

In every stage of these oppressions we have petitioned for redress in the most humble terms; our repeated petitions have been answered only by repeated injury. A prince whose character is thus marked by every act which may define a tyrant is unfit to be the ruler of a free people.

We have asked the king to end the unfair treatment of the colonies many times, but each time new abuses were added. A king who acts so unfairly is unfit to rule a free people.

Nor have we been wanting in attentions to our British brethren. We have warned them, from time to time, of attempts by their legislature to extend an unwarrantable jurisdiction over us. We have reminded them of the circumstances of our emigration and settlement here. We have appealed to their native justice and magnanimity; and we have conjured them, by the ties of our common kindred, to disavow these usurpations, which would inevitably interrupt our connections and correspondence. They, too, have been deaf to the voice of justice and of consanguinity. We must, therefore, acquiesce in the necessity which denounces our separation, and hold them, as we hold the rest of mankind, enemies in war, in peace, friends.

We have hoped the British people would help us end the abuses, so we sent many messages to them. We have told them how Parliament has mistreated us. The British people have not listened to our messages. Therefore, we must declare that we are a separate nation. We will treat Great Britain as we treat all other nations.

We, therefore, the representatives of the United States of America, in General Congress assembled, appealing to the Supreme Judge of the world for the rectitude of our intentions, do, in the name, and by authority of the good people of these colonies, solemnly publish and declare, that these united colonies are, and of right ought to be, free and independent states; that they are absolved from all allegiance to the British crown, and that all political connection between them and the state of Great Britain is, and ought to be, totally dissolved; and that as free and independent states, they have full power to levy war, conclude peace, contract alliances, establish commerce, and to do all other acts and things which independent states may of right do. And, for the support of this declaration, with a firm reliance on the protection of Divine Providence, we mutually pledge to each other our lives, our fortunes and our sacred honor.

As representatives of the people of the United States, we declare that these united colonies are one, independent nation. We have completely cut ties to Great Britain. As an independent nation, we have the right to wage war, make peace treaties, have trade with all nations, and do all the things a nation does.

We now trust that God will protect us. We promise to support this Declaration with our lives, our money, and our honor.

The Constitution of the United States

PREAMBLE ————————————

We, the people of the United States, in order to form a more perfect Union, establish justice, insure domestic tranquility, provide for the common defense, promote the general welfare, and secure the blessings of liberty to ourselves and our posterity, do ordain and establish this Constitution for the United States of America.

We, the people of the United States, want a better nation, so we are writing this plan of government, which has these five goals: create a justice system, encourage peace in the nation, defend the nation from its enemies, promote the well-being of the people, and protect the freedom of the people now and in future times.

The Framers began writing the Constitution in May 1787. On September 17, 1787, they signed it. The Preamble states the goals of the Constitution.

ARTICLE I. The Legislative Branch ————

Section 1. The Congress

All legislative powers herein granted shall be vested in a Congress of the United States, which shall consist of a Senate and a House of Representatives.

The power to make laws shall be given to Congress. Congress will have a Senate and a House of Representatives.

Section 2. The House of Representatives

The House of Representatives shall be composed of members chosen every second year by the people of the several states; and the electors in each state shall have the qualifications requisite for electors of the most numerous branch of the state legislature.

Members of the House of Representatives shall be elected by voters every two years. Each state decides its own voting requirements, but states must allow all people who vote for members of their state legislatures to vote for members of the House of Representatives.

According to the Fifteenth and Nineteenth Amendments, states cannot take away the right to vote because of race or sex.

No person shall be a Representative who shall not have attained the age of 25 years, and been seven years a citizen of the United States, and who shall not, when elected, be an inhabitant of that state in which he shall be chosen.

To be a member of the House of Representatives, a person must be an American citizen for at least seven years, be at least 25 years old, and live in the state he or she represents.

Representatives ~~and direct taxes~~ shall be apportioned among the several states which may be included within this Union, according to their respective numbers, ~~which shall be determined by adding to the whole number of free persons, including those bound to service for a term of years, and excluding Indians not taxed, three fifths of all other persons.~~ The actual enumeration shall be made within three years after the first meeting of the Congress of the United States, and within every subsequent term of ten years, in such manner as they shall by law direct. The number of Representatives shall not exceed one for every 30,000, but each state shall have at least one Representative; and until such enumeration shall be made, the state of New Hampshire shall be entitled to choose three, Massachusetts eight, Rhode Island and Providence Plantations one, Connecticut five, New York six, New Jersey four, Pennsylvania eight, Delaware one, Maryland six, Virginia ten, North Carolina five, South Carolina five, and Georgia three.

Representation for each state is based on

its population. Every state must have at least one representative. The population of each state must be counted in a census every ten years. The number of representatives from a state can change as the population changes.

The lines in the original Constitution were crossed out because they no longer apply. These lines explain how slaves were to be counted as a result of the Three-Fifths Compromise. The law was overturned by the Thirteenth Amendment of 1865, which ended slavery.

When vacancies happen in the representation from any state, the executive authority thereof shall issue writs of election to fill such vacancies.

When a seat becomes vacant in the House, it must be filled. The state governor must call a special election to fill the seat.

The House of Representatives shall choose their Speaker and other officers; and shall have the sole power of impeachment.

The members of the House must elect a Speaker and other officers. Only the House of Representatives has the power to impeach a member of the federal government.

Section 3. The Senate

The Senate of the United States shall be composed of two Senators from each state, chosen by the legislature thereof, for six years; and each Senator shall have one vote.

Each state shall send two senators that serve six-year terms to the Senate. These senators shall be chosen by the state legislatures.

As part of the Great Compromise, the Framers agreed that all states would have equal representation in the Senate, but representation in the House would be based on population. Since the 17th Amendment was added to the Constitution in 1913, all senators are elected by the voters in every state.

Immediately after they shall be assembled, in consequences of the first election, they shall be divided as equally as may be into three classes. The seats of the Senators of the first class shall be vacated at the expiration of the second year, of the second class at the expiration of the fourth year, and of the third class at the expiration of the sixth year, so that one third may be chosen every second year: and if vacancies happen by resignation, or otherwise, during the recess of the legislature of any state, the executive thereof may make temporary appointments until the next meeting of the legislature, which shall then fill such vacancies.

The senators were divided into three groups when they met for the first time in 1789. This was done so that one third of the senator seats would come up for election every two years, while the remaining two thirds of the senators would continue to serve.

The Senate, unlike the House, is a continuing body because only one third of its members are elected at a time.

No person shall be a Senator who shall not have attained the age of 30 years, and been nine years a citizen of the United States, and who shall not, when elected, be an inhabitant of that state for which he shall be chosen.

To be a United States senator, a person must be at least 30 years old, be a citizen for at least nine years, and live in the state he or she represents.

The Vice President of the United States shall be President of the Senate, but shall have no vote, unless they be equally divided.

The Vice President acts as president of the Senate. He or she can vote only to break a tie.

The Senate shall choose their other officers, and also a President *Pro Tempore*, in the absence of the Vice President, or when he shall exercise the office of President of the United States.

The senators shall elect officers to lead Senate meetings. One of these officers will be a President *pro tempore* who will lead the Senate when the Vice President cannot attend meetings.

The Senate shall have the sole power to try all impeachments. When sitting for that purpose, they shall be on oath or affirmation. When the President of the United States is tried, the Chief Justice shall preside: and no person shall be convicted without the concurrence of two thirds of the members present.

After the members of the House have voted to impeach a government leader, the impeachment trial can be held only by the Senate. The Chief Justice of the Supreme Court must preside at a trial of the President. A two-thirds vote is needed to convict a leader.

Judgment in cases of impeachment shall not extend further than to removal from office, and disqualification to hold and enjoy any office of honor, trust, or profit, under the United States; but the party convicted shall nevertheless be liable and subject to indictment, trial, judgment, and punishment according to law.

When a government leader is found guilty by the Senate, that leader is removed from office and is never allowed to hold another government office. This is the only way a person can be punished by the Senate. However, the guilty leader can be given a regular jury trial and receive punishment from a judge.

Since 1789, only seven people have been found guilty during Senate trials. They were removed from office but never put on trial before a regular court.

Section 4. Elections

The times, places, and manner of holding elections for Senators and Representatives, shall be prescribed in each state by the legislature thereof; but the Congress may at any time by law make or alter such regulations, except as to the places of choosing Senators.

State legislatures shall decide the places, times, and ways to hold elections for senators and representatives. Congress can make laws to change state decisions on the times and ways to hold elections. It cannot change state decisions on the places for holding elections.

All states hold elections for members of Congress on the first Tuesday after the first Monday in November of even-numbered years.

The Congress shall assemble at least once in every year, and such meeting shall be on the first Monday in December, unless they shall by law appoint a different day.

Congress must meet at least once a year.

Section 5. Meetings of Congress

Each House shall be the judge of the elections, returns, and qualifications of its own members, and a majority of each shall constitute a quorum to do business; but a smaller number may adjourn from day to day, and may be authorized to compel the attendance of absent members, in such manner, and under such penalties, as each House may provide.

Each house decides whether its members meet the qualifications that were stated in Sections 2 and 3 and whether they were legally elected. A quorum, or majority, of members must be present for each house to do business. Each house can decide on punishment for members who miss meetings.

Meetings are often held without a quorum, but a quorum is always needed when voting on a bill.

Each House may determine the rules of its proceedings, punish its members for disorderly behavior, and, with the concurrence of two thirds, expel a member.

Each house makes its own rules for running meetings and deciding how members who disobey rules should be punished. A house can expel one of its members with a two-thirds vote.

Each house has different rules for debates. These rules allow the Senate to have long debates and filibusters, while the House limits debating time.

Each House shall keep a journal of its proceedings, and from time to time publish the same, excepting such parts as may, in their judgment, require secrecy; and the yeas and nays of the members of either House on any question, shall, at the desire of one fifth of those present, be entered on the journal.

Each house shall publish a journal that tells what happened at each session. Secret information that affects the nation's security is not published. Voting records on bills are published when one fifth of the members vote for publication.

Congress' journal, *The Congressional Record*, can be found in public libraries.

Neither House, during the session of Congress, shall, without the consent of the other, adjourn for more than three days, nor to any other place than that in which the two Houses shall be sitting.

Both houses must agree on when to end a session for more than three days. Each house must always meet in the same place.

Section 6. Salaries and Rules

The Senators and Representatives shall receive a compensation for their services, to be ascertained by law, and paid out of the Treasury of the United States. They shall, in all cases, except treason, felony, and breach of the peace, be privileged from arrest during their attendance at the session of their respective Houses, and in going to, and returning from, the same; and for any speech or debate in either House, they shall not be questioned in any other place.

Members of Congress shall be paid salaries that are decided in laws passed by Congress. Salaries are paid from the nation's treasury. Members cannot be arrested while going to and from their work in Congress unless they commit serious crimes. They cannot be arrested for anything they say or write as part of their work during a session.

No Senator or Representative shall, during the time for which he was elected, be appointed to any civil office under the authority of the United States, which shall have been created, or the emoluments whereof shall have been increased during such time; and no person holding any office under the United States, shall be a member of either House during his continuance in office.

Members of Congress cannot be appointed to government jobs that were created or given a higher salary while they were in office. People cannot serve in Congress while they hold a government job.

This clause helps to keep a separation of powers.

Section 7. Bills

All bills for raising revenue shall originate in the House of Representatives; but the

Senate may propose or concur with amendments as on other bills.

All tax bills must start in the House of Representatives. After the bills are passed by the House, they are sent to the Senate. The Senate can approve or amend them.

Every bill which shall have passed the House of Representatives and the Senate, shall, before it become a law, be presented to the President of the United States; if he approves he shall sign it, but if not he shall return it, with his objections, to that House in which it shall have originated, who shall enter the objections at large on their journal, and proceed to reconsider it. If after such reconsideration two thirds of that House shall agree to pass the bill, it shall be sent, together with the objections, to the other House, by which it shall likewise be reconsidered, and if approved by two thirds of that House, it shall become a law. But in all such cases the votes of both Houses shall be determined by yeas and nays, and the names of the persons voting for and against the bill shall be entered on the journal of each House respectively. If any bill shall not be returned by the President within 10 days (Sundays excepted) after it shall have been presented to him, the same shall be a law in like manner as if he had signed it, unless the Congress by their adjournment prevent its return, in which case it shall not be a law.

Every bill that is passed by the House and Senate must then be read by the President. A bill becomes a law if the President signs it within ten days, not counting Sundays. If the President does not approve of the bill, he can veto it by returning the bill unsigned to the house that introduced it. Congress can override the President's veto if two thirds of the members of both houses vote for the bill. The Congressional Record must show how the members voted. A bill also becomes a law if the President holds it for ten days,

without counting Sundays, and does not sign it. If Congress adjourns and the President holds a bill without signing it for ten days, not counting Sundays, the bill cannot become a law. This last method of defeating a bill is called the pocket veto.

Every order, resolution, or vote, to which the concurrence of the Senate and House of Representatives may be necessary (except on a question of adjournment), shall be presented to the President of the United States; and before the same shall take effect, shall be approved by him, or being disapproved by him, shall be repassed by two thirds of the Senate and House of Representatives, according to the rules and limitations prescribed in the case of a bill.

Every order and joint resolution that is passed by both the Senate and the House needs the President's approval. The President must approve or veto resolutions just as he does bills.

Section 8. Powers of Congress
The Congress shall have power:

Congress shall have these powers:

To lay and collect taxes, duties, imposts, and excises, to pay the debts, and provide for the common defense and general welfare of the United States; but all duties, imposts, and excises shall be uniform throughout the United States;

To collect different kinds of taxes in order to pay for the nation's government and defense;
Federal taxes must be the same for every part of the nation.

To borrow money on the credit of the United States;

To borrow money;

The government borrows money by selling bonds. It must repay borrowed money.

To regulate commerce with foreign nations, and among the several states, and with the Indian tribes;

To control commerce with foreign nations, between the states of the nation, and with the Indian tribes;

Commerce means trade and business. This commerce clause allows Congress to pass all laws necessary for helping business between states. It also allows Congress to pass laws that control transportation between states.

To establish a uniform rule of naturalization, and uniform laws on the subject of bankruptcies throughout the United States;

To make laws on how people can become citizens; to pass laws about bankruptcy, or losing all of one's money, for the entire nation;

To coin money, regulate the value thereof, and of foreign coin, and fix the standard of weights and measures;

To print and coin money and decide how much that money is worth; to decide how much foreign money is worth in the United States; to set standards for weights and measures;

To provide for the punishment of counterfeiting the securities and current coin of the United States;

To make laws about punishing people who produce counterfeit money, stamps, and government bonds;

To establish post offices and post roads;

To set up post offices and create routes for delivering mail;

To promote the progress of science and useful arts, by securing, for limited times, to authors and inventors, the exclusive right to their respective writings and discoveries;

To promote art and science in the nation by issuing copyrights and patents;

To constitute tribunals inferior to the Supreme Court;

To create a system of lower federal courts;
The Framers planned the highest court, the Supreme Court, but gave Congress the job of planning all lower courts.

To define and punish piracies and felonies committed on the high seas, and offenses against the law of nations;

To punish crimes committed on the seas and against other nations;

To declare war, grant letters of marque and reprisal, and make rules concerning captures on land and water;

To declare war and issue letters of marque and reprisal;
The President can send troops to fight in any part of the world, but only Congress can declare war. Letters of marque and reprisal were documents issued to allow private ships to attack enemy ships. Since the Civil War, the United States has obeyed an international law that does not allow the use of letters of marque and reprisal.

To raise and support armies; but no appropriation of money to that use shall be for a longer term than two years;

To create and pay for an army; Congress can provide enough money to support the army for two years at a time;

This clause keeps the army under civilian control and limits its power. Since the army depends on Congress for money, it cannot become so powerful that it will take control of the government.

To provide and maintain a navy;

To provide and take care of a navy;

To make rules for the government and regulation of the land and naval forces;

To make rules for controlling the army and navy;

In 1950, Congress used this power to pass military laws called the Uniform Code of Military Justice. Since then, amendments have been added to that law.

To provide for calling forth the militia to execute the laws of the Union, suppress insurrections and repel invasions;

To call the militia, or National Guard, into action in order to carry out the nation's laws, put down riots and revolts, and fight against invading enemies;

To provide for organizing, arming, and disciplining the militia, and for governing such part of them as may be employed in the service of the United States, reserving to the states respectively, the appointment of the officers, and the authority of training the militia according to the discipline prescribed by Congress;

To make rules for organizing, controlling, and arming the state militia; states can appoint officers for the Guard, but all soldiers must be trained according to the laws of Congress;

Since the National Defense Act was passed in 1916, federal money has been used to help pay for the National Guard. The President can call on the National Guard to help during an emergency or to fight during a war.

To exercise exclusive legislation, in all cases whatsoever, over such district (not exceeding 10 miles square) as may, by cession of particular states, and the acceptance of Congress, become the seat of the government of the United States, and to exercise like authority over all places purchased by the consent of the legislature of the state in which the same shall be, for the erection of forts, magazines, arsenals, dockyards, and other needful buildings. And,

To make all laws for the District of Columbia, where the nation's capital is located; to make laws for land owned by the federal government;

This land includes national parks, forests, and post offices.

To make all laws which shall be necessary and proper for carrying into execution the foregoing powers, and all other powers vested by this Constitution in the government of the United States, or in any department or officer thereof.

To make all necessary laws so Congress can carry out the powers listed in the Constitution.

This clause is called the elastic clause because it allows Congress to write laws that are needed for a changing nation.

Section 9. Powers Not Given to Congress

The migration or importation of such persons as any of the states now existing shall think proper to admit, shall not be prohibited by the Congress prior to the year 1808; but a tax or duty may be imposed on such importation, not exceeding 10 dollars for each person.

Congress could not make laws to stop the slave trade until the year 1808.

This clause was one of compromises made by the Framers. In 1808, Congress passed a law that stopped the nation from importing slaves from Africa.

The privilege of the writ of *habeas corpus* shall not be suspended, unless when in cases of rebellion or invasion the public safety may require it.

Congress cannot take away the right of *habeas corpus* except if there is a revolution or war.

The writ of habeas corpus is a legal order that says a police officer or sheriff must appear before a judge with a person who is being held in jail. The judge decides whether the accused person is being held legally, and if not, the person must be released. The writ of habeas corpus protects people from being kept in jail without a fair trial.

No bill of attainder or *ex post facto* law shall be passed.

Congress cannot pass a bill of attainder or an *ex post facto* law.

This clause protects a person from being punished without a trial and from being punished for something that was made illegal after he or she did it.

No capitation, or other direct tax, shall be laid, unless in proportion to the census or enumeration herein before directed to be taken.

Congress cannot collect a tax on each person unless the tax is based on state populations in the last census.

This clause was changed by the Sixteenth Amendment in 1913. That amendment allows Congress to collect a direct tax on people's income.

No tax or duty shall be laid on articles exported from any state.

Congress cannot tax goods that are exported from one state to another.

No preference shall be given by any regulation of commerce or revenue to the ports of one state over those of another; nor shall vessels bound to, or from, one state be obliged to enter, clear, or pay duties in another.

Congress cannot favor any state when making laws to control trade between states. Ships shall not be taxed when they go from one state to another.

No money shall be drawn from the treasury, but in consequence of appropriations made by law; and a regular statement and account of the receipts and expenditures of all public money shall be published from time to time.

Federal money can only be spent to pay for legislation passed by Congress. It must publish records that show how money is spent.

The power of Congress to spend money is very important. The President can plan programs and policies, but only Congress can provide the money to pay for them.

No title of nobility shall be granted by the United States; and no person holding any office of profit or trust under them, shall, without the consent of the Congress, accept of any present, emolument, office, or title of any kind whatever, from any king, prince, or foreign state.

Congress is not allowed to give titles of nobility, such as prince, king, or duke, to any person. Members of the government cannot accept gifts or titles from foreign nations without permission from Congress.

This clause is based on the idea from the Declaration of Independence that all people are equal. The Framers did not want the nation to have a noble class of titled people who were more powerful and important than the rest of the population.

Section 10. Powers Not Given to the States

No state shall enter into any treaty, alliance, or confederation; grant letters of marque and reprisal; coin money; emit bills of credit; make any thing but gold and silver coin a tender in payment of debts; pass any bill of attainder, *ex post facto* law, or law impairing the obligation of contracts, or grant any title of nobility.

States shall not have the power to make treaties and alliances with foreign nations or to coin money. These powers belong to the federal government. Neither state nor federal governments have the power to pass bills of attainder and ex post facto laws or to grant titles of nobility.

No state shall, without the consent of the Congress, lay any imposts or duties on imports or exports, except what may be absolutely necessary for executing its inspection laws; and the net produce of all duties and imposts, laid by any state on imports or exports, shall be for the use of the Treasury of the United States; and all such laws shall be subject to the revision and control of the Congress.

States are not allowed to tax imported or exported goods without permission from Congress. They may charge a small fee for the inspection of goods that enter the state. If Congress does permit states to tax goods, the tax money must belong to the United States Treasury. These laws can be changed by Congress.

No state shall, without the consent of Congress, lay any duty of tonnage, keep troops, or ships of war, in time of peace, enter into any agreement or compact with another state, or with a foreign power, or engage in war, unless actually invaded, or in such imminent danger as will not admit of delay.

States cannot tax goods on ships. They cannot have their own army and navy, but they can have soldiers in the National Guard. States cannot make treaties or declare war against other nations.

Our system of federalism gives all powers of foreign policy and national defense to the federal government.

ARTICLE II. The Executive Branch

Section 1. President and Vice President

The executive power shall be vested in a President of the United States of America. He shall hold his office during the term of four years, and together with the Vice President, chosen for the same term, be elected as follows:

The executive power is given to a President of the United States. The President and the Vice President shall serve four-year terms.

Each state shall appoint, in such manner as the legislature thereof may direct, a number of electors equal to the whole number of Senators and Representatives to which the state may be entitled in the Congress; but no Senator or Representative, or person holding an office of trust or profit under the United States, shall be appointed an elector.

Each state shall choose a group of people called electors to elect the President. The number of electors from a state must equal the number of senators and representatives from that state. Members of Congress and other government officials cannot be electors.

The electors shall meet in their respective states, and vote by ballot for two persons, of whom one at least shall not be an inhabitant of the same state with themselves. And they shall make a list of all the persons voted for, and of the number of votes for each; which list they shall sign and certify, and transmit sealed to the seat of the government of the United States, directed to the President of the Senate. The President of the Senate shall, in the presence of the Senate and House of Representatives, open all the certificates, and the votes shall then be counted. The person having the greatest number of votes shall be the President, if such number be a majority of the whole number of electors appointed; and if there be more than one who have such majority, and have an equal number of votes, then the House of Representatives shall immediately choose by ballot one of them for President; and if no person have a majority, then from the five highest on the list the said House shall in like manner choose the President. But in choosing the President, the votes shall be taken by states, the representation from each state having one vote; a quorum for this purpose shall consist of a member or members from two thirds of the states, and a majority of all the states shall be necessary to a choice. In every case, after the choice of the President, the person having the greatest number of votes of the electors shall be the Vice President. But if there should remain two or more who have equal votes, the Senate shall choose from them by ballot the Vice President.

Clause 3 explains how to elect the President and Vice President. It was changed by the Twelfth Amendment, in 1804.

The Congress may determine the time of choosing the electors, and the day on which they shall give their votes; which day shall be the same throughout the United States.

Congress sets one date for choosing

electors and sets another date for electors to vote for President. The dates must be the same for the entire nation.

Electors are chosen every fourth year on Election Day, which is the first Tuesday after the first Monday in November.

No person except a natural-born citizen, or a citizen of the United States, at the time of the adoption of this Constitution, shall be eligible to the office of President; neither shall any person be eligible to that office who shall not have attained the age of 35 years, and been 14 years a resident within the United States.

To be President, a person must be a citizen who was born in the United States, be at least 35 years old, and live in the nation for at least 14 years.

In case of the removal of the President from office, or of his death, resignation, or inability to discharge the powers and duties of the said office, the same shall devolve on the Vice President, and the Congress may by law provide for the case of removal, death, resignation, or inability, both of the President and Vice President, declaring what officer shall then act as President, and such officer shall act accordingly until the disability be removed, or a President shall be elected.

The Vice President shall become the President if the nation's President dies, resigns, or is unable to work. Congress must decide who becomes President if the nation does not have a Vice President.

The Twenty-fifth Amendment tells when the Vice President becomes the President and how another person must then be chosen to be the new Vice President.

The President shall at stated times receive for his services a compensation, which shall neither be increased nor diminished during the period for which he shall have been elected, and he shall not receive within that period any other emolument from the United States or any of them.

The President shall receive a salary. The amount will be decided by Congress, and it cannot be changed while the President is in office. A President cannot receive money from any state or from any other part of the federal government while in office.

Before he enter on the execution of his office, he shall take the following oath or affirmation:

"I do solemnly swear (or affirm) that I will faithfully execute the office of President of the United States, and will, to the best of my ability, preserve, protect, and defend the Constitution of the United States."

On the day a President takes office, he must take the Presidential Oath. With this oath, the new President swears to carry out the duties of the presidency and to protect and defend the United States Constitution.

Section 2. President's Powers

The President shall be Commander in Chief of the Army and Navy of the United States, and of the militia of the several states, when called into the actual service of the United States; he may require the opinion, in writing, of the principal officer in each of the executive departments, upon any subject relating to the duties of their respective offices, and he shall have power to grant reprieves and pardons for offenses against the United States, except in cases of impeachment.

The President shall be the commander in chief of the army, navy, and National Guard. He may order the leaders of executive departments to report on their work. The President has the power to grant pardons for federal crimes. Pardons cannot be granted to a person who has been impeached.

This clause puts the military under civilian control. The clause also allows the President to create a cabinet with executive department leaders.

He shall have power, by and with the advice and consent of the Senate, to make treaties, provided two thirds of the Senators present concur; and he shall nominate, and by and with the advice and consent of the Senate, shall appoint ambassadors, other public ministers and consuls, judges of the Supreme Court, and all other officers of the United States, whose appointments are not herein otherwise provided for, and which shall be established by law. But the Congress may by law vest the appointment of such inferior officers, as they think proper, in the President alone, in the courts of law, or in the heads of departments.

The President can make treaties with foreign nations, but the treaties cannot be used unless two thirds of the senators vote for them. The President appoints ambassadors to foreign nations and judges to the Supreme Court. These appointments must receive a majority of votes in the Senate. The President can appoint people to less-important government offices. Senate approval is not needed for less-important positions.

This clause gives the President the power to make foreign policy. The Senate checks the President's power of making appointments.

The President shall have power to fill up all vacancies that may happen during the recess of the Senate, by granting commissions which shall expire at the end of their next session.

The President can appoint people to government jobs when the Senate is not in session. These jobs will be temporary, since the appointments were not approved by the Senate.

Section 3. Other Powers

He shall, from time to time, give to the Congress information of the state of the Union, and recommend to their consideration such measures as he shall judge necessary and expedient. He may on extraordinary occasions, convene both Houses, or either of them; and in case of disagreement between them, with respect to the time of adjournment, he may adjourn them to such time as he shall think proper. He shall receive ambassadors and other public ministers. He shall take care that the laws be faithfully executed; and shall commission all the Officers of the United States.

The President shall deliver a State of the Union address to both houses of Congress. When necessary, he shall recommend to Congress new laws that the nation needs. To deal with emergencies and serious problems, the President may call on Congress to meet in special sessions after it has adjourned. If the two houses cannot agree on when to adjourn, then the President shall decide when Congress shall adjourn. The President shall meet with ambassadors and leaders from other nations. The President must make sure the laws of Congress are carried out properly. The President gives federal officers the power to have their jobs and to do their responsibilities.

Planning the nation's budget is one of the President's major responsibilities. After the President prepares the budget, it must be passed by Congress. Congress checks the President's power because it can vote against the budget or not provide the money the President wants for new programs. Very few special sessions of Congress are called since Congress now meets for most of the year.

Section 4. Impeachment

The President, Vice President, and all civil officers of the United States, shall be removed from office on impeachment for, and conviction of, treason, bribery, or other high crimes and misdemeanors.

The President, Vice President, and all officers not in the military can be removed from office through impeachment. A President and other officials can be impeached for treason, or giving help to enemy nations, for bribery, and for committing crimes.

Andrew Johnson was the only President to be impeached. The Senate lacked one vote for the required two-thirds vote that was needed to find him guilty.

ARTICLE III. The Judicial Branch ———
Section 1. Judges

The judicial power of the United States shall be vested in one Supreme Court, and in such inferior courts as the Congress may, from time to time, ordain and establish. The judges, both of the Supreme and inferior courts, shall hold their offices during good behavior; and shall, at stated times, receive for their services, a compensation, which shall not be diminished during their continuance in office.

Judicial power is given to the Supreme Court and to lower courts that are set up by Congress. Judges of the Supreme Court and the lower federal courts are appointed for lifetime terms unless they are impeached for wrongdoing. Judges shall be paid salaries that cannot be lowered while they are in office.

The Framers wanted the courts to be separate from the other branches so that judges would not be pressured by Congress or the President to make unfair decisions.

Section 2. Federal Courts

The judicial power shall extend to all cases, in law and equity, arising under this Constitution, the laws of the United States, and treaties made, or which shall be made, under their authority; to all cases affecting ambassadors, other public ministers, and consuls: to all cases of admiralty and maritime jurisdiction; to controversies to which the United States shall be a party; to controversies between two or more states, ~~between a state and citizens of another state,~~ between citizens of different states, between citizens of the same state claiming lands under grants of different states, ~~and between a state, or the citizens thereof, and foreign states, citizens, or subjects.~~

Federal courts have the power to hear many different kinds of cases. They can hear all cases that deal with the Constitution, the laws of Congress, ambassadors, ships at sea, the actions of government leaders, problems between two states, and problems between citizens and their state.

The Eleventh Amendment, in 1798, changed this clause slightly. Only state governments can deal with problems between a state and citizens of another state or nation.

This clause gives the Supreme Court the power of judicial review, which is the right to overturn any law that is found unconstitutional. Judicial review is one of the most important powers of the Supreme Court. The Supreme Court used this power to overturn state segregation laws.

In all cases affecting ambassadors, other public ministers and consuls, and those in which a state shall be party, the Supreme Court shall have original jurisdiction. In all the other cases before mentioned, the Supreme Court shall have appellate jurisdiction, both as to law and fact, with such exceptions, and under such regulations, as the Congress shall make.

The Supreme Court has two kinds of jurisdiction, or power, to hear cases. It has original jurisdiction, which is the power to hear cases the first time they go to court; it has appellate jurisdiction, which is the power to hear cases that were decided in a lower court and appealed to the Supreme Court. The Supreme Court has original jurisdiction in cases that involve states or ambassadors. These cases are presented directly to the Supreme Court. Most cases that are heard by the Supreme Court have appellate jurisdiction. Congress can make rules about appealing cases to the Supreme Court.

The trial of all crimes, except in cases of impeachment, shall be by jury; and such trial shall be held in the state where the said crimes shall have been committed; but when not committed within any state, the trial shall be at such place or places as the Congress may by law have directed.

All cases dealing with federal crimes shall be decided by a jury trial in a federal court in the state where the crime was committed.

The right to a jury trial is one of the most important constitutional rights. It began with the Magna Carta in 1215. The Fifth and Sixth Amendments guarantee the rights of accused people.

Section 3. Treason

Treason against the United States, shall consist only in levying war against them, or in adhering to their enemies, giving them aid and comfort. No person shall be convicted of treason unless on the testimony of two witnesses to the same overt act, or on confession in open court.

A person commits treason against the United States by making war against the nation or by helping the enemies of the nation. A person can be convicted of treason only if two people state before a judge that they witnessed the same act of treason or if the person confesses to the crime in an open court.

The Congress shall have power to declare the punishment of treason, but no attainder of treason shall work corruption of blood, or forfeiture except during the life of the person attainted.

Congress has the power to make laws for the punishment of treason. Only the person who committed treason, and not the person's family, can be punished.

ARTICLE IV. Relations Between States ———
Section 1. Laws
Full faith and credit shall be given in each state to the public acts, records, and judicial proceedings of every other state. And the Congress may by general laws prescribe the manner in which such acts, records, and proceedings shall be proved, and the effect thereof.

Every state must respect the laws, records, and court decisions of every other state.

For example, every state has its own marriage laws. A marriage that takes place in one state is accepted in every other state.

Section 2. Citizens
The citizens of each state shall be entitled to all privileges and immunities of citizens in the several states.

When citizens visit another state, they must be given the same rights as the people of that state. States cannot treat citizens of other states unfairly.

A person charged in any state with treason, felony, or other crimes, who shall flee from justice, and be found in another state, shall, on demand of the executive authority of the state from which he fled, be delivered up to be removed to the state having jurisdiction of the crime.

If a person charged with a crime escapes to another state, that person must be found and returned to the state he or she ran away from.

Returning an accused person to the state or nation where the crime took place is called extradition.

No person held to service or labor in one state, under the laws thereof, escaping into another, shall, in consequence of any laws or regulation therein, be discharged from such service or labor, but shall be delivered up on claim of the party to whom such service or labor may be due.

This clause is about returning runaway slaves. This clause was overturned in 1865 by the Thirteenth Amendment, which ended slavery.

Section 3. States and Territories
New states may be admitted by the Congress into this Union; but no new state shall be formed or erected within the jurisdiction of any other state; nor any state be formed by the junction of two or more states or parts of states, without the consent of the legislatures of the states concerned, as well as of the Congress.

Congress has the power to admit new states to the Union. New states cannot be created by dividing one state or by joining two or more states unless the states and Congress agree.

Since 1787, 37 states have become part of the United States. They were all admitted to the Union by Congress. Five of them (Kentucky, Maine, Tennessee, Vermont, and West Virginia) were formed from older states, with their consent.

The Congress shall have power to dispose of and make all needful rules and regulations respecting the territory or other property belonging to the United States; and nothing in this Constitution shall be so construed as to prejudice any claims of the

United States, or of any particular state.

Congress shall make rules for selling and controlling federal property and territory.

Section 4. Protecting the States
The United States shall guarantee to every state in this Union a republican form of government, and shall protect each of them against invasion; and on application of the legislature, or of the executive (when the legislature cannot be convened), against domestic violence.

The United States guarantees that every state shall have a representative government. The federal government shall protect states from enemy invasions. If fighting and violence start in a state, the state legislature or governor can request help from the federal government.

ARTICLE V. Adding Amendments ————
The Congress, whenever two thirds of both Houses shall deem it necessary, shall propose amendments to this Constitution, or, on the application of the legislatures of two thirds of the several states, shall call a convention for proposing amendments, which, in either case, shall be valid to all intents and purposes, as part of this Constitution, when ratified by the legislatures of three fourths of the several states, or by conventions in three fourths thereof, as the one or the other mode of ratification may be proposed by the Congress; provided ~~that no amendment, which may be made prior to the year 1808, shall in any manner affect the first and fourth clauses in the ninth section of the first article; and~~ that no state, without its consent, shall be deprived of its equal suffrage in the Senate.

Amendments can be added to change the Constitution. The process to add amendments begins by proposing the new amendment. A proposal is made by a two-thirds vote for an amendment in both the Senate and House. One can also be made by two thirds of the state legislatures voting to have a national convention to propose an amendment. There are two ratification methods. Three fourths of the state legislatures must vote for the amendment, or three fourths of the state conventions must ratify it. Congress has the power to decide which method should be used for ratification.

Because the Framers made it difficult to add amendments, only twenty-six have been added to the Constitution. The Twenty-first Amendment was the only one ratified by state conventions. Amendments have allowed the Constitution to be a flexible document.

ARTICLE VI. The Supreme Law of the Land —
All debts contracted, and engagements entered into, before the adoption of this Constitution, shall be as valid against the United States, under this Constitution, as under the Confederation.

The United States government must repay debts on money that was borrowed before the Constitution was adopted.

The United States borrowed large amounts of money for the American Revolution and during the years after the war. The Framers wanted the money repaid so that people and other nations would trust the government of the new nation.

This Constitution, and the laws of the United States which shall be made in pursuance thereof, and all treaties made, or which shall be made, under the authority of the United States, shall be the supreme law of the land; and the judges, in every state, shall be bound thereby, anything in the constitution or laws of any state to the contrary notwithstanding.

The Constitution, the laws of Congress, and all treaties are the highest laws of the nation. State judges must understand that the United States Constitution is supreme over state laws.

This clause is called the Supremacy Clause. All state and local laws must agree with the Constitution. The Supreme Court can overturn laws that do not agree with the Constitution.

The Senators and Representatives before mentioned, and the members of the several state legislatures, and all executive and judicial officers, both of the United States and of the several states, shall be bound, by oath or affirmation, to support this Constitution; but no religious test shall ever be required as a qualification to any office or public trust under the United States.

All members of Congress, members of state legislatures, and all executive and judicial branch workers must take an oath and promise to obey the United States Constitution. There can be no religious requirements for people who apply for government jobs.

This clause shows the supremacy of the Constitution. Leaders of state and local governments must promise to obey the United States Constitution and to accept it as the highest law of the nation.

ARTICLE VII. Ratification——————————

The ratification of the conventions of nine states shall be sufficient for the establishment of this Constitution between the states so ratifying the same.

The Constitution will become the nation's law when nine states ratify it. Each state will hold a convention to vote on ratification.

The Constitution was signed by delegates from all twelve states at the Convention. It was signed on September 17, 1787. The nation became independent twelve years before the Constitution was written. Here are the names of the states and their delegates who signed:

George Washington,
President and Deputy from Virginia
Attest: William Jackson, Secretary

New Hampshire
John Langdon
Nicholas Gilman

Massachusetts
Nathaniel Gorham
Rufus King

Connecticut
William Samuel Johnson
Roger Sherman

New York
Alexander Hamilton

New Jersey
William Livingston
David Brearley
William Paterson
Jonathan Dayton

Pennsylvania
Benjamin Franklin
Thomas Mifflin
Robert Morris
George Clymer
Thomas Fitzsimmons
Jared Ingersoll
James Wilson
Gouverneur Morris

Delaware
George Read
Gunning Bedford, Jr.
John Dickinson
Richard Bassett
Jacob Broom

Maryland
James McHenry
Dan of St. Thomas Jennifer
Daniel Carroll

Virginia
John Blair
James Madison, Jr.

North Carolina
William Blount
Richard Dobbs Spaight
Hugh Williamson

South Carolina
John Rutledge
Charles Cotesworth Pinckney
Charles Pinckney
Pierce Butler

Georgia
William Few
Abraham Baldwin

The Constitution was ratified in 1788. Under the laws of this Constitution, Congress met for the first time in 1789. George Washington became the nation's first President in that same year.

AMENDMENTS

The first ten amendments are called the Bill of Rights. They were ratified on December 15, 1791.

AMENDMENT I. Freedom of Religion, Speech, Press, Assembly, and Petition

Congress shall make no law respecting an establishment of religion, or prohibiting the free exercise thereof; or abridging the freedom of speech, or of the press; or the right of the people peaceably to assemble, and to petition the government for a redress of grievances.

Congress cannot make laws to establish a religion for the nation. It cannot stop people from having freedom of religion. Congress cannot pass laws that take away freedom of speech, freedom of the press, or the right to assemble peacefully in groups. It cannot stop people from asking government leaders to correct something that the people think is wrong.

At the time the Bill of Rights was written, the United States was one of the first nations to allow freedom of religion. The separation of church and state clause in the First Amendment requires that religion be completely separate from the government. This differed from British law, which allowed an official religion that was supported with government money.

Americans use their First Amendment rights when they form groups that work for causes and when they write letters to government leaders. People are not allowed to use their rights to hurt others.

AMENDMENT II. The Right to Bear Arms

A well regulated militia being necessary to the security of a free state, the right of the people to keep and bear arms shall not be infringed.

Every state needs a well-armed militia to protect the people. The federal government cannot take away the right of the people to have guns.

State governments can pass laws to control the ownership of guns. The Second Amendment has been used to prevent Congress from passing gun control laws.

AMENDMENT III. The Housing of Soldiers

No soldier shall, in time of peace, be quartered in any house without the consent of the owner; nor in time of war, but in a manner to be prescribed by law.

People cannot be forced to have soldiers eat and sleep in their homes in peaceful times. In order for soldiers to stay in civilian homes during a war, Congress must pass a special law.

AMENDMENT IV. Search and Arrest

The right of the people to be secure in their persons, houses, papers, and effects, against unreasonable searches and seizures, shall not be violated; and no warrants shall issue, but upon probable cause, supported by oath or affirmation, and particularly describing the place to be searched, and the persons or things to be seized.

People have the right to be safe from police searches and arrests in their homes. Police are not allowed to search people or their homes, arrest people, or seize evidence without a court order or warrant from a judge. A judge can only issue a warrant for very good reasons. Evidence that is taken without a warrant cannot be used to convict a person.

AMENDMENT V. The Rights of Accused Persons

No person shall be held to answer for a capital or otherwise infamous crime, unless on a presentment or indictment of a grand jury, except in cases arising in the land or naval forces, or in the militia, when in actual service, in time of war or public danger; nor shall any person be subject for the same offenses to be twice put in jeopardy of life or limb; nor shall be compelled, in any criminal case, to be a witness against himself; nor be deprived of life, liberty, or property, without due process of law; nor shall private property be taken for public use without just compensation.

A person can stand trial for a capital crime or other serious crime only after being accused of the crime by a grand jury. A capital crime is a crime that can be punished with the death penalty. Once a jury decides that a person is not guilty, that person cannot be tried again for the same crime in the same court. This is known as double jeopardy. Accused people cannot be forced to speak or provide evidence against themselves. Every accused person has the right to due process. This means they must receive fair treatment according to the law. The government must pay a fair price to people when it takes private property for government use.

AMENDMENT VI. The Right to a Fair Trial

In all criminal prosecutions the accused shall enjoy the right to a speedy and public trial, by an impartial jury of the state and district wherein the crime shall have been committed, which district shall have been previously ascertained by law, and to be informed of the nature and cause of the accusation; to be confronted with the witnesses against him; to have compulsory process for obtaining witnesses in his favor; and to have the assistance of counsel for his defense.

Every accused person has the right to a speedy trial. The accused must be given a public trial by a fair jury. Accused people must be told what crimes they have been charged with. At the trial, they have the right to question witnesses who present evidence against them. Accused people can have their own witnesses with evidence to support their case. An accused person has the right to be defended in court by a lawyer.

The Framers believed in the importance of a speedy trial. They had seen how accused people in Britain were sometimes held in jail for a long time without a trial. Accused people have the right to a jury trial only when they say that they are innocent of the crime. A person who pleads guilty to a crime is sentenced by a judge and does not stand trial. The Sixth Amendment also gives accused people the right to a defense lawyer. In the 1963 case *Gideon v. Wainwright*, the Supreme Court decided that a person cannot receive a fair trial without a defense lawyer. Because of that decision, states must provide lawyers to all people who cannot pay for their own defense.

AMENDMENT VII. Civil Cases

In suits at common law, where the value in controversy shall exceed 20 dollars, the right of trial by jury shall be preserved; and no fact tried by a jury shall be otherwise re-examined in any court of the United States than according to the rules of the common law.

This amendment guarantees the right to a jury trial in civil cases that involve at least twenty dollars.

Civil cases are about problems between people, such as money, property, and divorce. Although the Seventh Amendment applies to federal courts, most states also allow jury trials for civil cases.

AMENDMENT VIII. Bail and Punishment

Excessive bail shall not be required, nor excessive fines imposed, nor cruel and unusual punishments inflicted.

Courts cannot ask accused people to pay unfair amounts of bail money. People cannot be punished with fines that are too high. A person who is found guilty should not be given a cruel or unfair punishment for the kind of crime committed.

Bail is money that a judge orders an accused person to give to the court. Bail money is held by the court until the trial and then returned when the accused person goes on trial. Since bail money is used to guarantee that the accused person will not run away, the money is not returned if the accused does not come to the trial. If an accused person cannot pay bail, that person must wait in jail until the trial begins. The Framers did not want the amount of bail to be so high that accused people would be forced to wait in jail for their trials.

AMENDMENT IX. Other Rights

The enumeration in the Constitution of certain rights shall not be construed to deny or disparage others retained by the people.

The Constitution explains certain rights that the government must protect. The people have many other important rights that are not listed in the Constitution, and those rights must be protected by the government.

AMENDMENT X. Powers Belonging to States

The powers not delegated to the United States by the Constitution, nor prohibited by it to the states, are reserved to the states respectively or to the people.

All of the powers that the Constitution did not give to the federal government and did not keep from the states belong to state governments and to their people.

When the Constitution was written, many people feared that the federal government would have too much power over the states. The Tenth Amendment showed that federalism allows both a strong federal government and separate state governments with many powers of their own.

AMENDMENT XI. Cases Against States (1798)

The judicial power of the United States shall not be construed to extend to any suit in law or equity, commenced or prosecuted against one of the United States by citizens of any state, or by citizens or subjects of any foreign state.

A state cannot be sued in a federal court by a citizen from another state or from a foreign nation.

AMENDMENT XII. Election of the President and Vice President (1804)

The electors shall meet in their respective states, and vote by ballot for President and Vice President, one of whom, at least, shall not be an inhabitant of the same state with themselves; they shall name in their ballots the person voted for as President, and in distinct ballots the person voted for as Vice President; and they shall make distinct lists of all persons voted for as President, and of all persons voted for as Vice President, and of the number of votes for each, which list they shall sign and certify, and transmit, sealed, to the seat of the government of the

United States, directed to the President of the Senate; the President of the Senate shall, in the presence of the Senate and House of Representatives, open all the certificates, and the votes shall then be counted. The person having the greatest number of votes for President shall be the President, if such number be a majority of the whole number of electors appointed; and if no person have such majority, then from the persons having the highest numbers, not exceeding three, on the list of those voted for as President, the House of Representatives shall choose immediately, by ballot, the President. But in choosing the President, the votes shall be taken by states, the representation from each state having one vote; a quorum for this purpose shall consist of a member or members from two thirds of the states, and a majority of all the states shall be necessary to a choice. And if the House of Representatives shall not choose a President whenever the right of choice shall devolve upon them, before the fourth day of March next following, then the Vice President shall act as President, as in the case of the death or other constitutional disability of the President. The person having the greatest number of votes as Vice President shall be the Vice President, if such number be a majority of the whole number of electors appointed; and if no person have a majority, then from the two highest numbers on the list the Senate shall choose the Vice President. A quorum for the purpose shall consist of two thirds of the whole number of Senators, and a majority of the whole number shall be necessary to a choice. But no person constitutionally ineligible to the office of President shall be eligible to that of Vice President of the United States.

To elect a President, electors shall meet in their own states and cast one ballot for a presidential candidate and another ballot for a vice-presidential candidate. When all electors have voted, the ballots are sent to the President of the United States Senate. The President of the Senate shall count the votes for each candidate in front of both houses of Congress. The presidential candidate with the greatest number of votes shall be President. The winning candidate must receive more than half of the electoral votes. If none of the candidates receive a majority of votes, then the House of Representatives must choose one of the candidates to be President. Each state is allowed only one vote when electing the President. At least two thirds of the states must cast votes. To be elected, a candidate must receive a majority of votes in the House. If the House does not choose a President by March 4, the Vice President shall act as President. (The date of March 4 was later changed to January 20.) The vice-presidential candidate with the greatest number of electoral votes shall be the Vice President. If none of the candidates receive a majority of votes, then the Senate shall choose the Vice President. Two thirds of the senators must vote. The candidate who receives a majority of votes shall be Vice President. The Vice President must meet the same constitutional requirements of age, residency, and citizenship as the President.

The Twelfth Amendment overturned the procedures for electing a President that were listed in Article 2, Section 1, Clause 3. Much of the presidential election process is not included in the Constitution. Thomas Jefferson and John Quincy Adams were the only presidents that were chosen by the House of Representatives.

AMENDMENT XIII. Slavery (1865)

Section 1. Neither slavery nor involuntary servitude, except as a punishment for a crime whereof the party shall have been duly convicted, shall exist within the United States, or any place subject to their jurisdiction.

Section 2. Congress shall have power to enforce this article by appropriate legislation.

This amendment ended slavery. It said that slavery shall not exist in the United States or in territories ruled by this nation. Forced labor can be used only as a punishment for crime. Congress shall have the power to make laws to carry out this amendment.

AMENDMENT XIV. Rights of Citizens (1868)

Section 1. All persons born or naturalized in the United States, and subject to the jurisdiction thereof, are citizens of the United States and of the state wherein they reside. No state shall make or enforce any law which shall abridge the privileges or immunities of citizens of the United States; nor shall any state deprive any person of life, liberty, or property, without due process of law, nor deny to any person within its jurisdiction the equal protection of the laws.

All people who are born or naturalized in the United States are citizens of both the nation and the state where they live. A naturalized citizen is a person who was born in a different nation, moved to the United States, and went through a legal process to become a citizen. States cannot make laws that take away the rights of citizens. States must give all people the right to due process. They cannot punish people by taking away their life, freedom, or property without due process. Every person in a state must be given equal protection by the laws.

The first sentence in this amendment gave citizenship to African Americans. The Fifth Amendment guaranteed due process to people accused of crimes by the federal government. The Fourteenth Amendment guarantees that state governments will also allow due process to all people. Many civil rights laws that have been passed by Congress are based on the Fourteenth Amendment. The equal protection clause was used by the Supreme Court when it ruled on the *Brown v. Topeka Board of Education*

case. The Supreme Court decided that separate schools for black and white children did not allow equal protection. That decision and the Fourteenth Amendment were used to overturn state segregation laws across the nation.

Section 2. Representatives shall be apportioned among the several states according to their respective numbers, counting the whole number of persons in each state, excluding Indians not taxed. But when the right to vote at any election for the choice of electors for President and Vice President of the United States, representatives in Congress, the executive and judicial officers of a state, or the members of the legislature thereof, is denied to any of the male inhabitants of such state, being 21 years of age, and citizens of the United States, or in anyway abridged, except for participation in rebellion or other crime, the basis of representation therein shall be reduced in the proportion which the number of such male citizens shall bear to the whole number of male citizens 21 years of age in such state.

The number of members from each state in the House of Representatives depends on the state's population. This clause overturned the Three-Fifths Compromise that was used in Article 1. This clause says that everyone is counted in the census except Indians, who are not taxed. States cannot take away the right to vote in state or federal elections unless a person has committed a serious crime. States that unfairly take away the right to vote will have fewer representatives in Congress. States must allow all men who are over the age of 21 to vote.

This amendment says states that take away voting rights can be punished by losing some of their representatives in Congress, but this punishment has never been used. Voting rights were given to women in the Nineteenth Amendment and to people as young as eighteen in the Twenty-sixth Amendment.

Section 3. No person shall be a Senator or Representative in Congress, or elector of President and Vice President, or hold any office, civil or military, under the United States, or under any state, who, having previously taken an oath, as a member of Congress, or as an officer of the United States, or as a member of any state legislature, or as an executive or judicial officer of any state, to support the Constitution of the United States, shall have engaged in insurrection or rebellion against the same, or given aid or comfort to the enemies thereof. But Congress may, by a vote of two thirds of each house, remove such disability.

This section was added to punish people who had been Confederate leaders during the Civil War. It says that they cannot hold office in the federal government. Congress can vote to remove this penalty.
In 1898, Congress removed this punishment for Confederate leaders.

Section 4. The validity of the public debt of the United States, authorized by law, including debts incurred for payment of pensions and bounties for services in suppressing insurrection or rebellion, shall not be questioned. But neither the United States nor any state shall assume or pay any debt or obligation incurred in aid of insurrection or rebellion against the United States, or any claim for the loss or emancipation of any slave; but all such debts, obligations, and claims shall be held illegal and void.

The United States is required by law to pay its debts on money borrowed for the Civil War. Neither the United States government nor the state governments are allowed to pay the war debts of the Confederate States. People who once owned slaves will not be paid for the loss of their slaves.

Section 5. The Congress shall have power to enforce, by appropriate legislation. the provisions of this article.

Congress shall have the power to make the laws that are needed to carry out this amendment.

AMENDMENT XV. Right to Vote (1870)
Section 1. The right of citizens of the United States to vote shall not be denied or abridged by the United States or by any state on account of race, color, or previous condition of servitude.

Citizens cannot be prevented from voting because of race, color, or because they have been slaves.

Section 2. The Congress shall have power to enforce this article by appropriate legislation.

Congress shall have the power to make laws to enforce this amendment.
The Fifteenth Amendment could only be carried out by laws of Congress. Many states passed laws that made it difficult for African Americans to vote. Martin Luther King, Jr., worked hard to win fair voting laws. His work influenced Congress, and in 1965, the Voting Rights Act was passed.

AMENDMENT XVI. Income Tax (1913)
The Congress shall have power to lay and collect taxes on incomes, from whatever source derived, without apportionment among the several states, and without regard to any census or enumeration.

Congress shall have the power to collect taxes on income. The amount of tax money collected does not depend on state populations.

Almost half of the money in the federal budget now comes from personal income taxes.

AMENDMENT XVII. Election of Senators (1913)

The Senate of the United States shall be composed of two Senators from each state, elected by the people thereof, for six years; and each Senator shall have one vote. The electors in each state shall have the qualifications requisite for electors of the most numerous branch of the state legislatures.

When vacancies happen in the representation of any state in the Senate, the executive authority of such state shall issue writs of election to fill such vacancies: Provided, That the legislature of any state may empower the executive thereof to make temporary appointments until the people fill the vacancies by election as the legislature may direct.

This amendment shall not be so construed as to effect the election or term of any Senator chosen before it becomes valid as part of the Constitution.

The United States Senate shall have two senators from each state. They shall be elected by the people of their states to serve six-year terms. Each senator shall have one vote. When there is a vacant seat in the Senate because a senator can no longer represent the state, the governor of that state shall call an election for a new senator. The state legislature can allow the governor to appoint a temporary senator, who will serve until the election takes place.

This amendment overturned the method of choosing senators that was discussed in Article 1, Section 3, Clauses 1 and 2 of the Constitution. Article 1 required that senators be elected by state legislatures. This amendment allows senators to be elected directly by the people in the same way that members of the House of Representatives are chosen. The amendment gives people a greater voice in government since they can choose their own representatives for both houses of Congress.

AMENDMENT XVIII. Prohibition of Liquor (1919)

Section 1. After one year from the ratification of this article the manufacture, sale, or transportation of intoxicating liquors within, the importation thereof into, or the exportation thereof from the United States and all territory subject to the jurisdiction thereof for beverage purposes is hereby prohibited.

One year after this amendment is ratified, liquor cannot be manufactured, sold, imported, or exported in the United States.

Section 2. The Congress and the several states shall have concurrent power to enforce this article by appropriate legislation.

Congress and the states have the power to make laws to enforce this amendment.

Section 3. This article shall be inoperative unless it shall have been ratified as an amendment to the Constitution by the legislatures of the several states, as provided in the Constitution, within seven years from the date of the submission hereof to the states by the Congress.

This amendment must be ratified within seven years or it cannot be part of the Constitution.

This amendment was repealed in 1933 by the Twenty-first Amendment. The laws against liquor were called Prohibition Laws. During the years of prohibition, a great deal of liquor was manufactured and sold illegally.

AMENDMENT XIX. Woman Suffrage (1920)

The right of citizens of the United States to vote shall not be denied or abridged by the United States or by any state on account of sex.

Congress shall have power to enforce this article by appropriate legislation.

Citizens of the United States shall not be prevented from voting because of their sex. Congress shall have the power to pass laws to carry out this amendment.

Wyoming was the first state to give women the right to vote in state elections. Later other states gave this right to women. But women in all states wanted to vote in national elections, so they worked for the woman suffrage amendment. From 1878 to 1918, an amendment on woman suffrage was proposed and defeated each year in Congress. Finally, the House approved the amendment in 1918, and the Senate did so in 1919. When it was ratified in 1920, woman had the right to vote in local, state, and national elections.

AMENDMENT XX. Lame Duck Amendment (1933)

Section 1. The terms of the President and Vice President shall end at noon on the 20th day of January, and the terms of Senators and Representatives at noon on the 3rd day of January, of the years in which such terms would have ended if this article had not been ratified; and the terms of their successors shall then begin.

The term of office of the President and Vice President shall end on January 20 at noon. The term of office for senators and representatives of Congress shall end on January 3 at noon. The new President and Vice President will take office on January 20. New members of Congress will take office on January 3.

Members of Congress who were defeated in the November elections are considered to have less power from that time until the new members are sworn in. These defeated members are called lame ducks. This amendment shortened the length of time a Lame Duck could remain in office.

Until this amendment, newly elected members did not begin work until March 4. This was so because when the Constitution was written, it took a long time for mail to reach the members and inform them of their new job. Then it took a while for them to travel to the capital to begin their work.

Section 2. The Congress shall assemble at least once in every year, and such meeting shall begin at noon on the 3rd day of January, unless they shall by law appoint a different day.

Congress shall meet at least once each year. The meetings shall begin on January 3 at noon.

Section 3. If, at the time fixed for the beginning of the term of the President, the President-elect shall have died, the Vice-President-elect shall become President. If a President shall not have been chosen before the time fixed for the beginning of his term, or if the President-elect shall have failed to qualify, then the Vice-President-elect shall act as President until a President shall have qualified; and the Congress may by law provide for the case wherein neither a President-elect nor a Vice President-elect shall have qualified, declaring who shall then act as President, or the manner in which one who is to act shall be selected, and such person shall act accordingly until a President or Vice President shall have qualified.

If the President-elect dies, the Vice-President-elect shall become the new President. If a new President has not been chosen before the time the new term is to begin, the Vice-President-elect will act as President. Congress can pass laws to decide who will be a temporary President if the nation does not have a President-elect or a Vice-President-elect.

This section discusses problems that have never happened in the history of the United States.

Section 4. The Congress may by law provide for the case of the death of any of the persons from whom the House of Representatives may choose a President whenever the right of choice shall have devolved upon them, and for the case of the death of any of the persons from whom the Senate may choose a Vice President whenever the right of choice shall have devolved upon them.

The Twelfth Amendment required the House of Representatives to choose a President if none of the presidential candidates received a majority of electoral votes. If one of the three presidential candidates dies, Congress can pass a law on how to choose a President. This also applied to the Vice President.

This situation has never occurred, and Congress has never had to pass this type of law.

Section 5. Sections 1 and 2 shall take effect on the 15th day of October following the ratification of this article.

After this amendment is ratified, Sections 1 and 2 will take effect on October 15.

Section 6. This article shall be inoperative unless it shall have been ratified as an amendment to the Constitution by the legislatures of three fourths of the several states within seven years from the date of its submission.

This amendment must be ratified within seven years by three fourths of the state legislatures.

AMENDMENT XXI. Repeal of the 18th Amendment (1933)

Section 1. The 18th article of amendment to the Constitution of the United States is hereby repealed.

The Eighteenth Amendment on prohibition is no longer a law of the United States.

Section 2. The transportation or importation into any state, territory, or possession of the United States for delivery or use therein of intoxicating liquors, in violation of the laws thereof, is hereby prohibited.

States can make their own laws about selling, transporting, or prohibiting liquor. It is a federal crime to disobey a state's liquor laws.

Section 3. This article shall be inoperative unless it shall have been ratified as an amendment to the Constitution by conventions in the several states, as provided in the Constitution, within seven years from the date of the submission hereof to the states by the Congress.

To become an amendment, this law must be ratified by state conventions within seven years.

The Twenty-first Amendment was the only amendment ratified by state conventions. Although Americans drank less liquor during the years the Prohibition Amendment was in effect, the amendment encouraged people to break the law in order to buy, sell, and manufacture liquor.

AMENDMENT XXII. Terms of the Presidency (1951)

Section 1. No person shall be elected to the office of the President more than twice, and no person who has held the office of President, or acted as President, for more than two years of a term to which some other person was elected President shall be elected to the office of the President more than once. But this article shall not apply to any person holding the office of President when this article was proposed by the Congress, and shall not prevent any person who may be holding the office of President, or acting as President, during the term within which this article becomes operative from holding the office of President or acting as President during the remainder of such term.

No person shall be elected to more than two terms of presidential office. A President who serves two years of another President's elected term can be elected to two more terms. A President shall not serve for more than ten years.

Section 2. This article shall be inoperative unless it shall have been ratified as an amendment to the Constitution by the legislatures of three fourths of the several States within seven years from the date of its submission to the States by Congress.

This amendment cannot be part of the Constitution unless it is ratified by three fourths of the state legislatures within seven years.

George Washington served only two terms of office. This tradition was followed by every President until Franklin D. Roosevelt was elected to four terms. Many Americans felt a President could become too powerful if he remained in office for more than ten years. So this amendment was added to the Constitution.

AMENDMENT XXIII. Voting in the District of Columbia (1961)

Section 1. The district constituting the seat of government of the United States shall appoint in such manner as the Congress may direct: A number of electors of President and Vice President equal to the whole number of Senators and Representatives in Congress to which the district would be entitled if it were a state, but in no event more than the least populous state; they shall be in addition to those appointed by the states, but they shall be considered, for the purposes of the election of the President and Vice President, to be electors appointed by a state; and they shall meet in the district and perform such duties as provided by the 12th article of amendment.

The people of the District of Columbia, as residents of the nation's capital and seat of government, shall vote for electors in presidential elections. The number of electors is to be the same as if the District of Columbia were a state. It cannot have more electors than the state with the smallest population. The electors shall help elect a President by following the rules of the Twelfth Amendment.

Section 2. The Congress shall have power to enforce this article by appropriate legislation.

Congress has the power to make laws to enforce this amendment.

Until 1961, citizens of Washington, D.C., could not vote in presidential elections. The District of Columbia is an area that is located between Maryland and Virginia. Since it is not a state, its citizens were not allowed to vote for President.

AMENDMENT XXIV. Poll Taxes (1964)

Section 1. The right of citizens of the United States to vote in any primary or other election for President or Vice President, for electors for President or Vice President, or for Senator or Representative in Congress, shall not be denied or abridged by the United States or any state by reason of failure to pay any poll tax or other tax.

It is the right of every citizen to vote in primary elections and presidential elections. Every citizen has the right to vote for senators and representatives in Congress. The federal and state governments cannot take away these rights because a person does not pay a poll tax or other kind of tax.

Section 2. The Congress shall have the power to enforce this article by appropriate legislation.

Congress has the power to make laws to enforce this amendment.

After the year 1889, eleven southern states had poll taxes. The poll-tax laws were used to prevent African Americans from voting. The Twenty-fourth Amendment said poll taxes could not be used to take away voting rights in federal elections. The amendment did not prevent states from having poll taxes for state and local elections. In 1966, the Supreme Court ruled that poll taxes were against the Equal Protection Clause of the Fourteenth Amendment. All poll taxes were declared unconstitutional, and they could no longer be used to stop people from voting.

AMENDMENT XXV. Presidential Succession (1967)

Section 1. In case of the removal of the President from office or his death or resignation, the Vice President shall become President.

The Vice President shall become President if the President dies, resigns, or is removed from office.

Section 2. Whenever there is a vacancy in the office of the Vice President, the President shall nominate a Vice President who shall take office upon confirmation by a majority vote of both houses of Congress.

Since the nation must have a Vice President, this office must be filled if it becomes vacant. The President shall nominate a person for Vice President. If a majority of senators and representatives vote for the nominated person, that person becomes the new Vice President.

Checks and balances are used since the House and Senate can check the President's choice for Vice President.

Section 3. Whenever the President transmits to the President *Pro Tempore* of the Senate and the Speaker of the House of Representatives his written declaration that he is unable to discharge the powers and duties of his office, and until he transmits to them a written declaration to the contrary, such powers and duties shall be discharged by the Vice President as Acting President.

If a President is unable to carry out his duties, he must write and tell the President *pro tempore* of the Senate and the Speaker of the House. Then the Vice President must be acting President until the President is able to work again.

In 1985, Vice President George Bush acted as President while Ronald Reagan had surgery.

Section 4. Whenever the Vice President and a majority of either the principal officers of the executive departments or of such other body as Congress may by law provide, transmit to the President *Pro Tempore* of the Senate and the Speaker of the House of Representatives their written declaration that the President is unable to discharge the powers and duties of his office, the Vice President shall immediately assume the powers and duties of the office as Acting President.

Thereafter, when the President transmits to the President *Pro Tempore* of the Senate and the Speaker of the House of Representatives his written declaration that no inability exists, he shall resume the powers and duties of his office unless the

Vice President and a majority of either the principal officers of the executive departments or of such other body as Congress may by law provide, transmit within four days to the President *Pro Tempore* of the Senate and the Speaker of the House of Representatives their written declaration that the President is unable to discharge the powers and duties of his office. Thereupon Congress shall decide the issue, assembling within 48 hours for that purpose if not in session. If the Congress, within 21 days after receipt of the latter written declaration, or, if Congress is not in session, within 21 days after Congress is required to assemble, determines by two-thirds vote of both houses that the President is unable to discharge the powers and duties of his office, the Vice President shall continue to discharge the same as Acting President; otherwise, the President shall resume the powers and duties of his office.

If the Vice President and a majority of cabinet leaders or Congress feels that the President is unable to carry out his duties, then they must tell this in writing to the President *pro tempore* and the Speaker of the House. Then the Vice President shall be acting President. Then, if the President writes that he is again able to carry out his duties, he will do so. However, the Vice-President and a majority of cabinet leaders can write declaring the President still unfit. Both houses must vote on the President's condition within 21 days. The Vice President will remain acting President if two thirds of the members of both houses vote for the Vice President. If there are not enough votes for the Vice President, the President can start to work again.

This amendment was added to make clear just what steps would be followed to decide whether the President is unable to carry out his duties. This was not made clear in Article 2, Section 1, Clause 6.

AMENDMENT XXVI. Voting Age of 18 (1971)

Section 1. The right of citizens of the United States, who are 18 years of age or older, to vote shall not be denied or abridged by the United States or by any state on account of age.

All citizens who are at least eighteen years of age shall be allowed to vote in state and federal elections.

Section 2. The Congress shall have power to enforce this article by appropriate legislation.

Congress shall have the power to pass laws to enforce this amendment.

The Constitution in 1787 gave the right to vote to white men. After the Civil War, the right to vote was given to African Americans. Then woman suffrage became law with the Nineteenth Amendment. Voting rights were given to the people of Washington, D.C., in 1961. Finally in 1971, the right to vote was given to eighteen-year-olds.

AMENDMENT XXVII. Congressional Pay (1992)

No law varying the compensation for the services of the Senators and Representatives shall take effect, until an election of Representatives shall have intervened.

Salary increases given to members of Congress will not take effect until after the next congressional election. This amendment prevents the members of Congress in session from giving themselves higher pay.

This amendment was originally introduced in 1789, but was not ratified for the Constitution by the necessary three fourths of the states until 1992.

Vocabulary List

Index